SCOTTISH ESTATE TWEEDS

THIRD EDITION

Published in 2018 by
Johnstons of Elgin
Newill, Elgin,
Moray IV30 4AF
Scotland
www.johnstonscashmere.com

Acknowledgements

I would like to thank the following for their assistance with this book:
HM The Queen; HRH The Duke of Rothesay; the estates, for giving us
permission to include their tweed; all those who sent us photographs for
inclusion; Sarah Wynn, for the administration, always done with a smile; Janet
Rae, for invaluable advice; all at Johnstons of Elgin; Iain Thornber, for his
wide knowledge of estates in the west of Scotland; Michael Gates Fleming
of Glenlyon Tweed Mill, who gave us samples, and guidance on estates; Islay
Tweed Mill and Campbell's of Beauly, who gave us samples; Regimental
Associations; Tailors; The Heritage Centre at Elgin Library; Lt-Col GS
Johnston; Innes Rankin of Inverness; John Innes and all at Think Publishing,
who have been so patient and a great help; and many more people.

Photography on the inside front and inside back covers

From top left to bottom right: Starting with Alexander Johnston who
established Johnstons in 1797 then showing all chairmen to the present day.
Next we show modern use of estate tweed, a bag and detailing on a shoe.
Photographs from Johnstons archives, Mark Williamson, Angus Bremner and
Holly Blake. Unless otherwise stated, images of tweed have been supplied by
their respective estates.

Designed by Think Publishing
33 Dalmarnock Road, Glasgow G40 4LA
Printed by TJ International

ISBN 978-0-9525329-2-7

GLEN TANAR TWEED BY ARAMINTA CAMPBELL

Children wearing
Kellas Estate Tweed

CONTENTS

Ian Urquhart (author, right) with his
son and daughter, Neil and Jenny
Urquhart, examining a historical ledger

PREFACE

Researching the estates of Scotland has been a fascinating project. Some estates have had their own distinctive tweed since the 1840s and each estate has its own story to tell. The 'Lovat Mixture', a tweed blend woven by Johnstons in 1845 for Lord Lovat, was the forerunner of the drab military uniform. At the same time, Lord Elcho designed the Hodden Grey Tweed. Lord Elcho clothed his London Scottish Regiment in what became known as Elcho Mixture, which was the origin of the khaki, the camouflage cloth worn by the British Army and then armies throughout the world. The first tweed check woven by Johnstons in 1846, the Coigach, became so popular in the United States that it was adopted by a gun club. It was such a seminal design that thereafter it was known as the 'gun club'.

The origins of estate tweeds are peculiarly Scottish, though their use has spread far beyond our border. A few English estates have developed the concept as have branches of the military. Examples of both are included in this book as they were in the original edition by Edward Stroud Harrison, published in 1968.

'ES' was my late wife's grandfather, and his son, Edward Paton Harrison, her father. Edward Paton Harrison, known as Ned, wrote the second edition of estate tweeds published in 1994/5. ES and Ned were chairmen of Johnstons of Elgin and now, as the firm's current chairman, it falls on me to update the book. Johnstons of Elgin is a family business owned by the grandchildren of ES Harrison.

The management and development of Scottish estates has changed considerably since the introduction of the first estate tweed. In recent years, many estates have invested heavily in buildings and infrastructure. Some now use power from their own hydro-electric schemes. Others practice forest sustainability. All provide employment and contribute to their local economies, most of which are in rural locations.

I am grateful to the many estate owners who have kindly supplied us with information and samples of their tweeds, and given us permission to reproduce their tweeds in this book. Thanks must also go to Glenlyon Tweed Mill, Islay Woollen Mill and Campbell's of Beauly who have given us samples and helped us make contact with estate owners. The designs included in this book are copyrighted to individual estates and must not be copied without permission. I am sure there are tweeds we have not been able to locate. Perhaps we will learn of these in due course and include them in the next edition of the book.

Johnstons of Elgin, established in 1797, continues to weave estate tweeds from wool although the weaving of these traditional cloths is now only part of our business. In 1851, not long after we began weaving estate tweeds, we became the first UK mill to weave cashmere and cashmere is now the major part of our production.

We started as a small, local woollen mill in Elgin and now employ around one thousand people. Our knitwear mill in Hawick, started in 1980, has contributed to this growth and to our successful export business. This book is a tribute to the highly talented and skilled people who work in our mills, as well as the other woollen mills in Scotland.

Ian Urquhart
Chairman
Johnstons of Elgin
Newmill, Elgin

HRH THE PRINCE CHARLES, DUKE OF ROTHESAY

I can only congratulate Johnstons of Elgin on the publication of the third edition of "Estate Tweeds". These distinctive woollen cloths, first called 'district checks', have been woven by the company since 1846. They represent a continuing tradition of social and economic history most often associated with the Highlands.

My great great great grandparents, Queen Victoria and Prince Albert were among the first to use distinctive estate tweed as clothing for the many workers on the Balmoral Estate. After purchasing the estate in 1852, Prince Albert designed both a Balmoral tartan and an estate tweed, which was woven by Johnstons of Elgin in 1853.

Unlike tartans which universally denote a clan, estate tweeds relate to a specific area of land. Socially, they unify the people who work on that land, but they also have a practical purpose. The colourings of the cloth were initially chosen to act as camouflage, allowing the wearer to blend in to their surroundings. Thus the more than 200 estate tweeds in this book also reflect the variety of colourings in the Scottish landscape – from the grey granite of Balmoral to the red, green and blue of the Northern Highlands. Each tweed is unique to the estate it was designed for.

The tradition of using distinctive tweeds continues to the present day for the many landowners who employ skilled workers to run their estates. The estate tweeds themselves also celebrate generations of talented designers and weavers, whose craft has flourished for almost two centuries and whose tweeds I am proud to wear myself.

THE HISTORY

THE HISTORY

The defeat of the Jacobite uprising led by Bonnie Prince Charlie at the Battle of Culloden Moor on 16 April 1746 was a watershed in Scottish history. After Culloden Highland society changed due to military defeat, laws and legislation, and most of all because of economic pressure.

The origin and story of estate tweeds can be found in those changes. Tweeds can be seen as a strand, albeit a small one, of Scottish social history. To understand that history, it is necessary to look at Highland society before the 1745 uprising.

Originally Highland society was tribal: it was based on a clan system which placed the chief at the apex.

Clan chiefs occupied a semi-regal position. Below them came the tacksmen, their closest kin. The chief was the main landowner while the tacksmen acted as viceroys over tracts of the chief's territories. They were also officers in the clan regiment and were often known by the name of the territory they held. Macdonald of Borrodale, for example, guarded this privilege with fierce pride. Many tacksmen were insignificant in their poverty but some attained the status of semi-chieftains in their own domain.

The **MacNeills of Barra** for example, claimed the titular right to sit down to dinner before any prince on earth. They were tacksmen to Macdonald of the Isles and paid an annual rent of forty cows and a peregrine falcon. Some tacksmen were farmers, most were also rentiers and, like the chiefs or proprietors, they sublet land to the tenants below them. The tenants were the principal landholders and they lived together in small townships across the Highlands. Below these tenants were a landless class of cotters, mailers or crofters who worked for the tenants and had the right to keep a cow and cultivate a small strip of land one day a week.

Clan society was held together by the myth of a common ancestor. A typical chief was male and most of his clan lived on his lands or those of his chieftains.

This society was patriarchal, involving an iron combination of duty and devotion. This duty worked both upwards and downwards. Tacksmen and tenants owed rent and service to the chief, but the chief also had an obligation to help and support members of the clan in times of hardship. In essence it was a military or martial society. Rents were often paid in kind and military service was a traditional form of payment.

Macdonell of Keppoch, one of two clan chiefs to be killed at Culloden, had boasted that his rent roll consisted of five hundred fighting men. Military service was a payment easily enforceable when the security of land tenure depended on the goodwill of the chief or tacksman.

This pattern of life, on the face of it so timeless and unchanging, was altering even

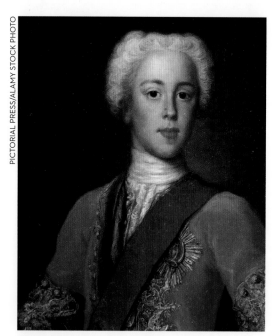

PICTORIAL PRESS/ALAMY STOCK PHOTO

Charles Edward Stuart (1720 to 1788), Jacobite pretender to the throne of Great Britain

as early as 1700. Sixty years had then passed since a young chief in the Western Isles led a raid on his neighbour's lands as an initiation into manhood.

The influence of the Lowlands was starting to cross the Highland line. The Highlands differed from the Lowlands because of the clan system, the language (Gaelic), religion and commercial activity. Such differences were gradually being eroded but progress was infinitely slow.

After the 1745 uprising the pace of this change accelerated sharply. The Jacobite rebellion had revealed the ultimate futility of the Highland appeal to arms. Once that had gone, there was little to stop the clan system disintegrating completely. The five thousand men raised to fight for Bonnie Prince Charlie were defeated in battle; legislation then consolidated the work of the army across the Highlands.

After his tour of the Hebrides in 1787, Samuel Johnson wrote: "There was never perhaps any change of national manners so quick, so great and so general, as that which has operated in the Highlands by the last conquest and subsequent laws. We came too late to see what we expected a people of peculiar appearance and a system of antiquated life. The clans retain little now of their original character: their ferocity of temper is softened, their military ardour is extinguished, their dignity of independence is depressed, their contempt of government is subdued, and their reverence for their chiefs is abated. Of what they had before the late conquest of their country there remains only their language and their poverty."

Culloden and its aftermath changed everything; the old Highlands receded into a mist of romance they had done little to deserve.

The most important factor to come into play was economic. One of the traditional Highland practices had been cattle stealing known euphemistically as lifting. Cattle were money. When law and order was brought to the Highlands cattle stealing was eradicated and cattle ranching became a worthwhile occupation.

The **1746 Act of Prohibition** was passed after the 1745 rebellion forbade men and boys in Scotland to wear tartan and Highland clothes, and to carry arms. Cattle drovers, however, were exempt from this latter prohibition.

Economic circumstances in the rest of Scotland and England in the last half of the eighteenth century changed enormously. The agricultural reforms of the late eighteenth century meant that the land could support a much larger population. Industries sprang up, creating wealth, and this economic expansion was probably more important than Culloden in the break up of Highland society.

Increasing prosperity manifested itself in the north as a rising demand for Highland products brought promise of material rewards to the exploiter of Highland resources on an unparalleled scale. Black cattle were the main export, with oatmeal the main import. In the fifty years between 1740 and 1790 the price of black cattle tripled while the price of oats did not even double.

Furthermore the introduction of the potato, a crop that would grow on marginal land in the years after 1760, meant that far fewer oats were needed to feed the population. The potato rapidly became the staple diet of the Highlanders.

At the same time, the price of wool began to rise and from 1760 onwards it was apparent that the Highlands could provide grazing grounds for the Cheviot and black-faced sheep from the south. In 1782 Sir John Lockhart-Ross became the first Highland landlord to lease grazing pastures for sheep when he let the land at Balnagowan to Thomas Geddes, a lowland sheep farmer. The following year Thomas Gillespie rented a sheep walk at Glen Quoich from Macdonell of Glengarry.

While black cattle could be accommodated within the traditional peasant economy of the Highlands, sheep could not. Sheep require large tracts of land to graze, in particular those hillsides the Highlanders had relied on to feed their cattle each summer. Sheep led to a basic change in land tenure.

Ironically the first class to suffer from the changing economic circumstances was the tacksmen, the nearest relatives of the chiefs.

ROSA BONHEUR - THE HIGHLAND SHEPHERD

The controversial Highland Clearances led to many landowners being dispossessed

> **"Culloden and its aftermath changed everything; the old Highlands receded into a mist of romance they had done little to deserve"**

Ruins of the former spinning mill at Spinningdale in Sutherland against the Dornoch Firth

When the trade in black cattle expanded, chiefs found that southern graziers were prepared to pay higher rents to run their cattle on the land previously rented to the tacksmen.

This prompted the first emigrations. In the nineteen years between 1772 and 1791, sixteen ships carrying about 6,400 people sailed from Inverness and Ross for Canada, Nova Scotia and the States. These were orderly exits compared with the miserable departures over the next fifty years and were often organised by tacksmen themselves who took their tenants with them.

The first large clearance from the Glengarry estates in the west took place in 1785, followed by large emigrations to Canada from Knoydart the following year. The first clearances in Sutherland took place in 1800, where small numbers of tenants were moved from their holdings on the north of the River Oykel.

For a time the Highlands were sheltered from the harshest economic changes. The price of black cattle remained high throughout the Napoleonic wars.

Two industries sprang up, both of which were labour intensive: kelp farming in the Western Isles and herring fishing on the west coast and in Sutherland. These absorbed some

of the tenants who had been removed from their land. There seemed grounds for optimism.

The Royal Highland and Agricultural Society of Scotland was founded in 1784 and residents talked of bringing industry to the Highlands. A mill was built at Spinningdale in Sutherland to compete with the woollen industry of Yorkshire and the Borders. Purpose-built villages were created at Ullapool, Beauly and elsewhere to promote the new herring fisheries. This occurred despite the view held by the developers that "the common people are lazy, ignorant and addicted to drinking."

It seemed reasonable to expect society to develop along Lowland lines, where the agricultural reforms of the eighteenth century had created a class of wealthy indigenous farmers with a landless class of labourers who worked for them.

Lowland Scotland was generally prosperous and such development did indeed take place in areas such as Aberdeenshire, Banffshire and around Inverness. But it didn't happen in the north and west where society became dominated by large numbers of tenants holding small parcels of land in crowded conditions. The peasant society of the clan was replaced by a different form of peasant society based on the smallholding. The tragedy of the Highlands during the first half of the nineteenth century is encapsulated within this scene.

At a time when the population was rising the economy collapsed. After 1815 cattle lost their value, the price of kelp fell from £20 (£1,300) a ton in 1808 to £3 (£240) a ton by 1830, by which time it was no longer worth gathering, and the herring moved from the inland lochs to the open seas where larger boats and more expensive equipment were required to harvest them. Only wool remained.

In 1792 Sir John Sinclair of Ulster brought the first Cheviot sheep to Sutherland. In 1795 he wrote: "The Highlands of Scotland may sell, at present, perhaps from £200,000 (£11,700,000) to £300,000 (£17,600,000) worth of lean cattle per annum. The same ground under sheep will produce twice as much mutton and there is wool into the bargain. If covered with the coarse-woolled breed of sheep, the wool might be worth about £300,000 (£17,600,000), the value of which can only be doubled by the art of the manufacturer; whereas the same ground under the Cheviot or True Mountain breed will produce at least £900,000 (£52,700,000) of fine wool."

The traditional Cheviot sheep of the Borders had been transformed in the middle of the eighteenth century by a farmer called

WORLD HISTORY ARCHIVE/ALAMY STOCK PHOTO

John Sinclair of Ulster (1754 to 1835), Scottish politician, economist and writer on finance and agriculture, born in Thurso

Robson. Robson mated his native ewes with rams from Lincolnshire and Spain, and within twenty years he created a breed of sheep which yielded a third more meat and wool, and which showed considerable stamina in the harsh winters of the Highlands. Land which produced 2d (1p) an acre under cattle produced 2s (6p) under sheep.

The economics of sheep farming spelled the end of the Highlands and made the clearances, the cause célèbre of Highland history, inevitable. Sir John Sinclair had pleaded with all landowners for a gradual, enlightened introduction of the Cheviot but the pace of change was too fast. Between 1807 and 1821 between five and ten thousand people were cleared from their homes in Sutherland alone to make way for sheep. Nowhere is the evidence more plainly seen than in Strathnaver.

Any tourist driving along Loch Naver today will come, at the foot of the loch, to Achness on the hillside on the other

"The economics of sheep farming spelled the end of the Highlands and made the clearances, the cause célèbre of Highland history, inevitable"

side of the river. There the grey stones of the former houses can be seen clearly beside the cemetery. The grass around them remains a brighter green, evidence of former cultivation.

Three miles further down the river on the Red Brae there is a monument erected to stonemason Donald Macleod, author of the *History of the Destitution in Sutherlandshire* and *Gloomy Memories*. The monument stands on the left bank of the river and looks across to the site of the former township of Rossall where Macleod was born and from where he was evicted by lawyer, Patrick Sellar in June 1814.

There is no doubt that the outrage felt at the thought of the clearances is due to Macleod. He conducted a lifelong crusade against Sellar as well as James Loch, the commissioner of the Stafford Estates. Loch was also the main architect behind the 'improvements' carried out on these estates throughout Sutherland.

"Every imaginable means," he wrote, "short of the sword or the musket, was put in requisition to drive the natives away, to force them to exchange their farms and comfortable habitations, erected by themselves or their forefathers, for inhospitable rocks on the seashore, and to depend for subsistence on the watery element in its wildest mood ... The country was darkened by the smoke of the burnings, and the descendants were ruined, trampled upon, dispersed and compelled."

Thirty-five years later he wrote even more searingly of the clearances from the Western Isles: "Hear the sobbing, sighing and throbbing, see the confusion, hear the noise, the bitter weeping and bustle. Hear mothers and children asking fathers and husbands, 'where are we going?' Hear the reply '*chan eil fhios agam*', 'we know not'."

With the benefit of hindsight it is necessary to see the events of the Sutherland clearances in a wider perspective. There can be no doubt that the condition of Sutherland at the beginning of the nineteenth century was primitive and backward. Stafford and Loch spent vast sums of money carrying out various schemes throughout the county in an attempt to create industry and wealth.

In 1820 Loch published *An Account of the Improvements on the Estate of Sutherland* belonging to the Marquess and Marchioness of Stafford. The book contains a chronicle of his policies and catalogues the improvements made in Sutherland during the previous seven years.

UK CITY IMAGES/ALAMY STOCK PHOTO

Above: The ruined remains of the Highland Clearances settlement at Grumbeg, with Loch Naver in the background

The HMS Hercules departs from the Isle of Skye in January 1853 bound for Adelaide, Australia

IAN G DAGNALL/ALAMY STOCK PHOTO

Portrait of Scottish novelist Sir Walter Scott (1771 to 1832) by Henry Raeburn, oil on canvas, 1822

Half a million pounds (22,700 kilos) of wool being exported annually; ninety miles of roads were being built; bridges were being constructed at Dornoch and Helmsdale; coal was being mined at Brora; the herring fishery at Helmsdale was established, £14,000 (£950,000) was invested in creating a modern port at Helmsdale alone. The list is impressive.

Unfortunately the pressures seen in Sutherland were common to the rest of the north and west of the Highlands. The scenes in Strathnaver were echoed over the next thirty years in Strathnoykel, Glencalvie, Strathconon, Glenelg and across the Western Isles. Emigration was, in effect, the only answer, as a growing population, a decaying economy, recurrent famine (the harvest failed in 1836, potato blight came from Ireland in 1846 and the crop failed again in 1850) and bitter poverty made exile inevitable.

In 1851, the Skye Emigration Society was founded, following the report prepared for the Home Secretary by Sir John MacNeill. The Highland and Island Emigration Society was formed a year later under the patronage of Prince Albert. The clearances of the Western Isles made sure that the sheep stations in Australia and New Zealand did not lack for shepherds.

Part of the tragedy of the Highlands in the nineteenth century originated in the first emigrations of the tacksmen in the last part of the eighteenth century. They were the people who might have formed the entrepreneurial class in society from which new ideas, new wealth and industry might have sprung. Without them there was less chance. Many of the chiefs were spendthrift and feckless. Few ploughed any money back into their estates and, when their revenues fell away, poverty and destitution forced them to sell.

The character deficiencies of these chiefs was one of the reasons why estate tweeds were designed and created in the nineteenth century. Another factor was the rediscovery of Scotland itself, the Scotland of the Waverley novels and Highland romance. There can be no doubt that Sir Walter Scott popularised the legend of Scotland and with it the recreation of the tartans of the clans.

In the introduction to the first edition of this book, published under the title *Our Scottish District Checks*, Edward Stroud Harrison wrote: "It would almost be true to say that he [Scott] was, if not their only begetter, at least the creator of their modern use. The tartans had their apotheosis in that enthusiastic fortnight in August of 1822 when George IV visited Edinburgh. Sir Walter was one of the chief hosts at the banquet in the ancient Parliament Hall at which the City entertained the King. Certainly, in the most truly glorious manner, the tartan cult was then launched with a flourish that probably neither before nor since has been accorded to any fashion. Certainly it resulted in one of the most truly magnificent collections of national designs ever brought together."

While tartans have little in common with estate tweeds in the design sense it is certainly true that if there had been no tartans there would have been no estate tweeds.

Queen Victoria and Prince Albert adopted the Highlands in the middle of the nineteenth century, contributing to the growing popularity of the area. After renting Balmoral estate from 1848, Prince Albert bought the estate in 1852 from the Farquharsons of Inverey. The foundation stone of Balmoral Castle was laid on 28 September 1853.

One of the first things Prince Albert did was to design the Balmoral Tartan and then a tweed for use by the stalkers and ghillies on the estate. It is one of the first true estate tweeds, of a dark blue design with white sprinkled with crimson. It appears to be grey overall and closely imitates the texture and effect of the granite mountains of Aberdeenshire around Balmoral. It was designed to provide camouflage while stalking in the Aberdeenshire hills.

Many of the English aristocracy followed their monarch to Scotland in the nineteenth century and Scottish estates were readily come by. Many of the Highland lairds, in particular those who lived on the west coast, wished to cut figures in society. Social life in Georgian and Regency times demanded money. Fortunes were won and lost on the gaming tables, and the income from the estates was insufficient to support the dignity required of a Highland chief.

Many estates were sold, some changing hands several times within

> **"There can be no doubt that Sir Walter Scott popularised the legend of Scotland and with it the recreation of the tartans of the clans"**

WORLD HISTORY ARCHIVE/ALAMY STOCK PHOTO

Queen Victoria (1819 to 1901) and Prince Albert (1819 to 1861) visiting the Highlands; Balmoral tweed and tartan

Glenmuick
Estate

thirty or forty years. The greatest sale came between 1813 and 1838 when Ranald George Macdonald of Clanranald, eighteenth captain of the clan, sold all his estates from Moidart to Arisaig on the mainland to South Uist in the Isles for £214,000 (£14,500,000). He retained only the island and castle of Tirrim.

General Roderick Macneil of Barra sold his island for £42,050 (£3,100,000) in 1839 and Colonel Gordon of Cluny bought it the next year for £38,050 (£2,700,000). Mackenzie of Seaforth bought Lewis for £160,000 (£10,500,000) in 1825 and sold it twenty years later for £190,000 (£16,200,000).

Grouse shooting and deer stalking became popular and this was helped, oddly enough, by the increase in the importation of wool from Australia. The Cheviot sheep did not retain its profitability during the nineteenth century and many lairds found they could augment their incomes by letting the stalking and fishing on their estates to southerners. A brace of grouse was the accepted unit of value; a brace was worth 5s (£18.00) and a salmon was worth twenty brace of grouse. By 1841 ninety Highland estates had shooting tenants each paying £125 (£8,900) a month or more.

The *Inverness Courier* commented: "This new branch of trade or commerce has added greatly to the rental of many estates. Instances are not rare of the shooting letting being as high as the grazing of a mountain district."

The literature of deer stalking also spread the popularity of the Highlands. The Sobieski Stuarts, the two imposters who gently let it be known that they were the grandsons of Bonnie Prince Charlie and were rowed down the Beauly to mass each Sunday with the Royal Standard flying at the stern of their barge, lived for several years on the island of Eilean Aigas, lent to them by Lord Lovat.

There they wrote *Vestiarium Scoticum* (*The Costumes of the Clans*), *Tales of the Century* and *Lays of the Deer Forest*, which was published in two volumes in 1848. William Scrope, neighbour of Sir Walter Scott on the Tweed, had published *Deer Stalking* ten years earlier. Landseer, Ansdell and other artists painted the Highlands and the red deer in a romantic light.

Allan Gordon Cameron in *The Wild Red Deer of Scotland* wrote in poetic terms of the change from sheep to deer: "Sheep-runs cleared of sheep became *ipso facto* deer-runs, and from old association were called deer-forests, even though completely denuded of wood. The passion for deer and the hills which had inspired the poetry of the Gaels, caught fire afresh from

> **"Deer stalking, salmon fishing and grouse shooting required professionals who could initiate the amateur into the craft of forest, moor, loch and river"**

the high tops of Athole, and at the call of Scrope, the chase of the hill stag instantaneously gripped the imagination of the sporting world."

Roads and railways were built, old lodges were refurbished, communication improved. Sport provided employment in the glens where: "as ghillies and stalkers ... dispossessed clansmen could once more pursue the sport of deer slaying which had been the joyful recreation of their forefathers for centuries."

Deer stalking, salmon fishing and grouse shooting required professionals who could initiate the amateur into the craft of forest, moor, loch and river. Each estate had its complement of retainers and it became the custom to dress all the men of an estate in one pattern of tweed. Such tradition endures in the twenty-first century.

THE DEVELOPMENT

To some extent, estate tweeds might be distant cousins of clan tartans. Both tweeds and tartans identify a group of people but while a tartan identifies members of the same family no matter where they live, estate tweeds identify people who live and work in the same area whether they are related or not.

Estate tweeds started as a Scottish phenomenon but they have spread to other countries. They are quite modern (the first estate tweeds were created in the 1840s) but it is often surprisingly difficult to trace their origins. Many of the individual patterns and districts, as opposed to estate tweeds such as the Glen Lyon, are particularly elusive in this respect. Many small mills were involved in producing them, although Ballantyne of Walkerburn and Johnstons of Elgin were the two primary suppliers. However, even at Johnstons, where the main archives covering the nineteenth century have survived, only the patterns exist without comment or history. It is a pity that no one set down chapter and verse at the time.

The development of estate tweeds was largely due to the decline in the influence of the clan chiefs and landowners in the Highlands. They were seduced by the social life in Edinburgh and London but found that their estates would not support them in the style enjoyed by the southern aristocracy. At the same time they found many people were anxious to follow the example of Queen Victoria and Prince Albert, and own or rent a sporting estate or deer forest.

In the Highlands, it was traditional for chiefs to provide clothing for their retainers. New tenants and owners wanted

to follow this example but had no right to wear a tartan. The first estate tweed, the Glenfeshie, is a good illustration of this. Between 1834 and 1841, General Balfour of Balbirnie and the Rt Hon Edward Ellice MP rented the Glenfeshie estate, which belonged to Sir George MacPherson-Grant.

According to her son, Miss Balfour (the General's daughter), was: "Disturbed because she had no tartan so she designed the check which Mr Ellice and the ghillies and keepers all wore from that day to the present." The design was a simple variant of the Shepherd Check.

In about 1770, Campbell of Combie brought John Tod from Dumbarton to tend his sheep. Later, a second shepherd, Braidfoot, brought another lot of Cheviots north. Border shepherds wore the traditional shepherd's plaid, a black-and-white check made from about six threads of black and six of white. Miss Balfour varied this pattern by superimposing a scarlet overcheck which gave her a 'tartan' for her staff. History has it that she adopted this design because the colours imitated the grey and red granites of the mountains around Glenfeshie but it seems more likely that she changed the design to distinguish the men of the forest from the shepherds.

Estate tweeds also provided useful camouflage for stalkers. To look at the Glenfeshie, Coigach or Dacre, it might appear to accomplish the opposite but it is surprising how effective many of the brightest tweeds are at breaking up a man's outline from a distance.

"The Glenurquhart design is possibly the most famous contribution to the fashion world by the Scottish tweed industry"

In most cases the colours chosen blended well with the mountains and moors in a specific area. The choice of tweed for Strathconon is a good example of this. Mr Peter Combe, whose family used to own the estate, found among his grandfather's effects a group of patterns which proved to be eight variations on the old Strathconon tweed. These dated from the time when his grandfather and the weaver were experimenting to find the most suitable blend. The different patterns were produced and the stalkers were sent up a hill with sample lengths while his grandfather sat on the front porch with his glass to see which tweed was the least visible.

The late Lord Lovat, too, related how his grandfather had pointed out to his wife that the colours on the far shore of Loch Morar – the sands, heather, bracken, bluebells and birches – blended to produce one beautiful colour effect. From this blend the original Lovat mixture was created.

SIR THOMAS LAWRENCE/FINE ARTS MUSEUMS OF SAN FRANCISCO

Left: Charlotte Georgina Jerningham, later Lady Lovat
Above: an example of Lovat tweed

Broadly speaking, the designs used in estate tweeds fall into four groups. The first follows the example set by Miss Balfour and uses variations on the Shepherd Check (see **page 132**). This includes designs which are based on the Coigach (**page 56**), known as gun clubs. The second uses variations of the Glenurquhart (**page 89**), while the third is based on tartan-type designs. The fourth uses a number of plain grounds with or without overchecks – this forms the group from which the camouflage uniform evolved.

In the first group, the Glenfeshie (**page 82**) is the simplest design but many of the tweeds vary the colour of the black and white, and introduce overchecks. The gun club designs are an adaptation of the Shepherd Check; the white ground is retained but the black is alternated with another colour. The Coigach was probably the first design to do this – in about 1870 it was adopted by one of the American

gun clubs (either New York or Baltimore) as their club colours. The style was then re-exported back to Britain and became known as a gun club.

The Glenurquhart design, the second group, is possibly the most famous contribution to the fashion world by the Scottish tweed industry. The original design was adopted by Caroline, Countess of Seafield for her estate at Glenurquhart.

Lady Seafield was a handloom weaver who has been credited with the design but it is more likely that it was created by Elizabeth Macdougall of Lewiston, a little village at the foot of the glen where it opens out to Loch Ness. William Fraser, the local weaver who was to produce the cloth, could not understand Elizabeth's instructions so she scratched the pattern on the ground at his cottage door with a stick. The pattern itself is a derivative of the Shepherd and is made up of blocks of small checks, usually four threads of white and four of a colour, alternated with a stripe effect of two and two in the same colours. The original Glenurquhart was woven in dark navy blue and white but this was later changed to white.

The third group of estate tweed designs had no particular feature. The last group is based on a plain ground, sometimes made with marled yarn, where two or more colours are twisted together before weaving. More usually, however, it's based on a mixture where wools dyed to different shades are blended before spinning to become one colour. Often these designs have overchecks.

The original mixture was no doubt the Lovat (**page 119**), which was first woven by Johnstons of Elgin on 26 September 1845 for MacDougalls of Inverness and invoiced as Lord Lovat's Mixture. The story behind the creation of Lovat tweed is told in detail in the section on individual tweeds but it is worth noting that this coincided with the development of the Hodden Grey tweed designed by Lord Elcho. He was raising the London Scottish Regiment at the time and thought it wrong that soldiers should be clad in so conspicuous a colour as scarlet. Lord Elcho clothed his regiment in a cloth which blended white and claret brown,

An 1860 engraving of Lord Elcho

"In estate tweeds the actual colours are important and should match as closely as possible"

which produced an effect similar to the red-brown soil of East Lothian.

This cloth, which is now more usually known as the Elcho Mixture, was the origin of the khaki worn by the British army and thus Lord Elcho can claim his uniform as the beginning of all the camouflage uniforms of armies around the world.

In estate tweeds the actual colours are important and should match as closely as possible. In this they differ from tartans where all colour variations are acceptable as long as they conform to the basic colour. For instance green can be a light or dark shade or any variation thereof.

However it is becoming increasingly difficult to match the original colours as most estate tweeds rely on one or more mixture yarns for their effect. Mixtures are more trouble and more costly to produce as they require the mill to hold various colours of wool. This used to be common practice in the first half of the twentieth century when most Scottish mills would accept an order for a single 50-yard piece of cloth.

Most mills nowadays still have a weaving minimum of one 60-metre piece of cloth. Any estate wanting to copy the old tweed might have to accept a slight change in colours as fewer mixtures are kept in stock.

Nevertheless it is still possible to make up patterns of the old estate tweeds. The creation of more than one hundred and fifty new tweeds since the first edition of this book in 1968 shows this is still a thriving industry.

There is one thing that would not be possible to emulate nowadays without the artifice of dyeing. Several of the old designs were made with what was known as laid whites, such as the Green Mar. Laid whites came from sheep which had been anointed with a mixture of tar and tallow or butter to protect them and their wool supposedly from the severity of the winter weather. Not surprisingly the mixture always stained the wool to a deep cream shade and the fleeces were marketed as laid. Instructions on the treatment of sheep with tar and tallow can be found in John Luccock's *Essay on Wool*, 1809 and Bakewell's *Observations on Wool*, 1808.

The practice was abandoned in England and the Borders quite early on, therefore the patterns based on the Shepherd Check used a pure white while those of Highland origin did not necessarily do so. Many of the colours have changed over the years as a number of the designs are now nearly one hundred and seventy years old.

Traditionally the dye used was based on vegetable matter and small lots were dyed in a variety of shades without any consistent quality control. Nowadays, the dyes produce a constant colour. The laid fleeces were awkward to work and much of the weight of the fleece was lost in scouring. There is a verse in an old Scottish ballad which mentions this difficulty.

Tarry'oo, tarry 'oo
Tarry 'oo is ill to spin:
Caird it weel, caird it weel
Caird it weel or ye begin.

When it's cairded, rowed and spun
Then the wark is halflins dune;
When it's woven, dressed and clean,
It micht be cleidith for a Queen.

'oo = wool; ill = difficult; caird = card; wark = work; cleidith = cloth

This concludes the history and development, and we now move to the tweeds themselves.

Shepherds Check: a Border farmer dressed in his 'Sunday Best' with his 'dress' plaid over his left shoulder and his 'nibby' stick in his right hand

Photograph taken by Allan Robinson, Arcade Hawick, early 1900s

ESTATE TWEEDS PAST AND PRESENT

PHOTOGRAPHY BY MARK WILLIAMSON

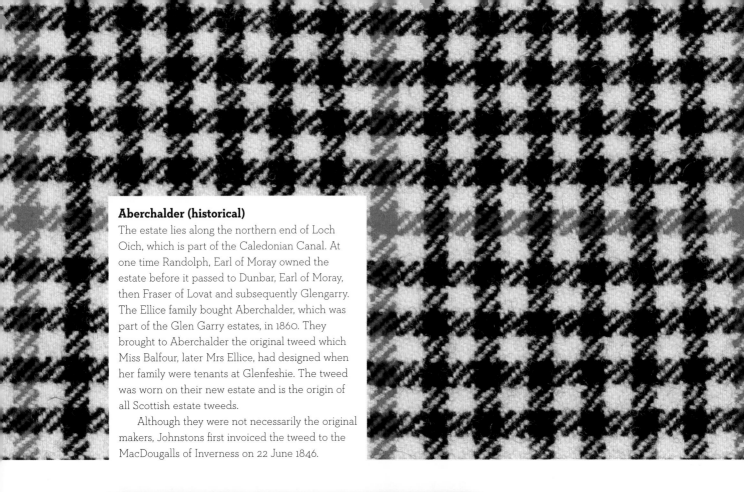

Aberchalder (historical)

The estate lies along the northern end of Loch Oich, which is part of the Caledonian Canal. At one time Randolph, Earl of Moray owned the estate before it passed to Dunbar, Earl of Moray, then Fraser of Lovat and subsequently Glengarry. The Ellice family bought Aberchalder, which was part of the Glen Garry estates, in 1860. They brought to Aberchalder the original tweed which Miss Balfour, later Mrs Ellice, had designed when her family were tenants at Glenfeshie. The tweed was worn on their new estate and is the origin of all Scottish estate tweeds.

Although they were not necessarily the original makers, Johnstons first invoiced the tweed to the MacDougalls of Inverness on 22 June 1846.

Alvie and Dalraddy

The estate lies four miles south of Aviemore near the village of Kincraig and extends from the River Spey into the Monadhliath Hills. Sir John Ramsden purchased Alvie estate in about 1865, planting 2,000 acres of trees before buying Ardverikie estate. Alvie was subsequently sold to Sir Robert Whitehead who fenced in much of the estate to ranch red deer. Lady Carnarvon purchased the estate in 1923, selling it to the Williamson family in 1927. The Williamson family purchased the adjoining Dalraddy estate in 1930.

The MacPherson-Grants of Ballindalloch are descendants of George MacPherson of Dalraddy estate. Subsequent purchases by the Williamson family include Invereshie, Blackmill, Ballintean and Balnespick farms in Glenfeshie. The Williamson family were involved in establishing and developing downhill skiing in the Cairngorms, Glenfeshie Gliding Club and Dalraddy Holiday Park. Today they have extensive sporting facilities.

The tweed has been used since 2006 and is woven by Johnstons.

NORTH AFFRIC

SOUTH AFFRIC

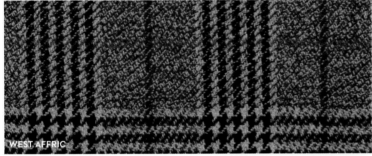

WEST AFFRIC

North Affric and South Affric (historical)

The estate lies in Glen Affric forty miles south-west of Inverness. The Chisholm originally owned Affric estate but Highland Estates Ltd took it over in the late 1920s to develop water power.

The estate was sold to Robert Wotherspoon, Lord Provost of Inverness, when Tom Johnston nationalised the power scheme. In 1950 Provost Wotherspoon sold the estate to the Forestry Commission but retained the lodge and sporting rights. Mr and Mrs Iain Wotherspoon took over the lodge and sporting rights in 1960 and bought back the northern part of the estate in 1983. Part of this was sold to John Watson in 1990 and then to David Matthews.

The estate is now divided into three parts: South Affric, which is owned by the Forestry Commission, West Affric owned by the National Trust and North Affric owned by Mr Matthews. There is some doubt as to who designed the brown tweed used by the Wotherspoon family. It may have been Lord Furness who was a sporting tenant during the 1920s and 30s. The green tweed was adopted by Mr Wotherspoon as being more suitable for the hill. It is not known if the tweed is still used.

Altries

The estate lies about nine miles south-west of Aberdeen and is currently owned by Melfort Campbell. Lt-Col Robert Campbell and Lt-Col Alastair Campbell OBE, DL owned the property previously. Lt-Col Alastair Campbell and Johnstons of Elgin designed the tweed in 1953.

The pattern is basically Shepherd Check but is varied by using a different pair of colours for warp and weft, resulting in a soft Lovat effect. Like many estate tweeds the colours have altered with changing manufacturers and the present version is somewhat lighter compared with the original.

Altyre

Altyre lies two miles south of Forres in Moray and is owned by the Gordon Cumming family. Sir Alastair Gordon Cumming had taken over the estate from his father Sir William Gordon.

The tweed design was introduced in about 1926 by Sir Alastair of Altyre and Gordonstoun. It is a slight variant of the basic Shepherd Check in that there is a slight difference between the warp and weft light colour and it is overchecked in blue. It was made by Hunters of Brora.

Altyre was one of the estates which features in the deer-stalking classic *Wild Sports of the Highlands* by Charles St John.

Ardtalla

The estate lies in the south-east corner of the Isle of Islay, just off the west coast of Scotland, and belongs to Ardtalla Estates Ltd.

Haggart's of Aberfeldy designed and produced the tweed, which was introduced to the estate by Jack Mactaggart in about 1958. Glenlyon Tweed Mill now manufactures it.

The Ramsay family owned the estate in the second half of the nineteenth century, who sold it to the Clifton family early in the 1900s. The Mactaggarts acquired the estate in parcels between 1952 and 1958.

Ardtalnaig

Ardtalnaig is twelve miles west of Aberfeldy and is owned by The Moncrieff Farm Partnership. Before that it belonged to the Berry Family Trust and the tweed depicted is that one. Not obvious in the illustration is the quiet russet overchecking in the weft which is dominated by the warp check. Glenlyon Tweed Mill manufacturers the tweed.

Ardtornish

The estate lies about fifteen miles north-west of Oban on the sound of Mull and is held in a trust by members of the Raven family. They bought the estate from the late Gerard Craig Sellar in 1930. Before that the Smith family owned it, who were ship's chandlers and distillers from London.

The design is a simple brown-and-white Shepherd Check. The shade, which has varied on occasion, was first produced by Johnstons in 1905 and supplied to George Harrison of Edinburgh. In later versions, the check is bigger as shown here.

Ardverikie

The estate lies about sixteen miles west of Newtonmore on the southern shores of Loch Laggan and is owned by the descendants of Sir John Ramsden who introduced the tweed in about 1920. Haggart's of Aberfeldy first produced it.

Sir John built Ardverikie House in 1873 and it is still used by his family. In ancient times the land belonged to the Cluny MacPhersons. The Marquis of Abercorn leased the estate from Cluny MacPherson and entertained Queen Victoria there on her first official visit to the Highlands in 1847. The design is a fairly small Glenurquhart only seven centimetres in the repeat.

Ardvorlich

The estate lies on the south side of Loch Earn, thirty miles west of Perth. The Stewarts of Ardvorlich have owned the property since the sixteenth century – the present owner is Alexander Stewart of Ardvorlich. Hunters of Brora designed the tweed and the present owner's father introduced it to the estate in about 1965.

Ardverikie Estate

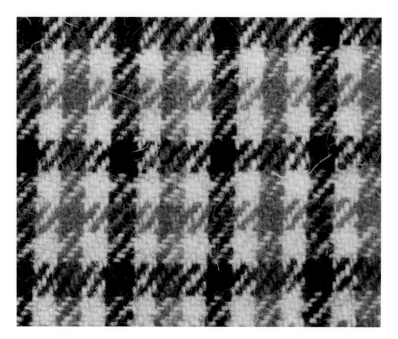

Arndilly

The estate lies along the River Spey, ten miles south-south-west of Elgin near the village of Craigellachie. Mr W Stuart Menzies, who owned the estate in 1933, is said to have copied the tweed from an old shooting coat that belonged to his father, Ronald Stuart Menzies of Culdares. He thought that the design probably evolved at Meggernie Castle in Glen Lyon in about 1870. The tweed is unusual, being a gun club with differing warp and weft, and an additional overcheck. The tweed is used today.

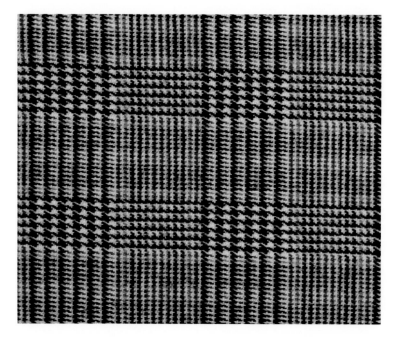

Old Athole or Atholl (historical)

The Atholl estates are in Perthshire, ten miles north-west of Pitlochry, and are owned by the Blair Charitable Trust. The earls and dukes of Atholl were part owners. There is no documentation about this tweed but Johnstons certainly produced it about one hundred and seventy years ago. It is a rather unusual treatment of the Glenurquhart check with regard to the elaborate red overchecking on the 2 x 2 section. It is no longer in use.

Atholl

This new form of Atholl check
replaced the older design in 1962.
It is a traditional gun club with
a combination of white and pale
Lovat for the light shades and a stronger
Lovat, russet and a strong mossy tone
for the darker colours. The whole
effect is beautiful and is almost
invisible on the hill.

Auch

The estate lies fifty miles south of
Fort William at the Bridge of Orchy.
It now belongs to Auch Farming Vehicle
Limited. Originally Auch was part of the
Breadalbane lands and was owned by the
Marchioness of Breadalbane. Mr Tadcastle
and Mr Braid Aitken have since owned
it. The design of the tweed comes from
Peter MacLennan of Fort William and
was introduced in about 1974.

Auchleeks

The estate is located at the west end of Glen Errochty, some ten miles west of Blair Atholl in Perthshire. Mr IJ Mackinlay introduced the tweed to the estate in its present form in 1965. There is no record of a previous design and it is still in use. The design uses a plain ground with overchecks.

Auchnafree

Auchnafree lies at the head of Glenalmond some twenty miles west-north-west of Perth. It is owned by the Whitaker family. The tweed was designed in 1992 by Janet Whitaker. It is still in use today and woven by Glenlyon Tweed Mill.

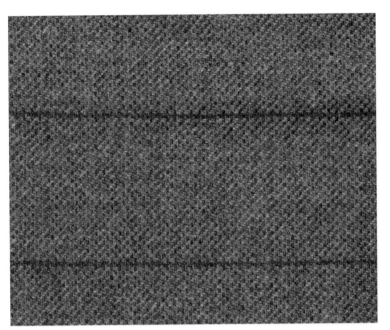

Badanloch

Badanloch is located in Sutherland, about 22 miles north-west of Helmsdale. The estate belongs to the Leverhulme Trust. Lord Leverhulme introduced the tweed to the estate in 1954 and it is in regular use. The design is a little unusual in that the weft checking is much stronger than the warp check, a reversal of the normal practice.

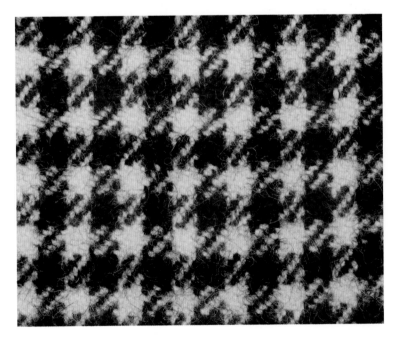

Baillie (historical)

There is some doubt about the origins of the Baillie. It was used for many years by Lord Burton at the Dochfour Estate along Loch Ness but it has now been replaced by the Glenquoich. In the old days the Baillies of Dochfour also owned the estate of Eilanreach on the west coast and the pattern may have originated there. In the Johnstons Day Book there is an entry dated 10 November 1857 for the supply of Baillie but there is nothing to indicate that they are the original makers.

Balavil

Balavil estate lies to the north of Kingussie and is set in the Monadhliath mountains. James MacPherson, translator of the *Ossian* poems, purchased the estate in 1790. It was then passed down to Allan and Marjorie MacPherson-Fletcher of Balavil. They sold the estate in 2015 but retained the tweed for their family's use and kept part of the estate to build themselves a more modest property.

Hunters of Brora first designed the tweed. Marjorie MacPherson-Fletcher later modified it before introducing it to the estate in 1970.

Balavil has a long history of shooting and stalking. Colonel Thornton rented the estate in the 1780s while on his famous sporting tour of the Highlands.

James MacPherson employed Robert Adam to build a grand mansion incorporating the Castle of Raits, a Mackintosh stronghold dating back to the 16th century.

BALLINDALLOCH HEAVY

BALLINDALLOCH LIGHT

Ballindalloch

Ballindalloch estate of Strathspey has been the family home of the MacPherson-Grant family since at least 1457 and lies about fifteen miles south-west of Elgin. Guy and Victoria MacPherson-Grant now live in Ballindalloch Castle with their family.

The tweed is derived from the Shepherd Check with a quiet green overcheck and has varied greatly in tone over the years. It is unusual in that the warp and weft light colours are slightly different. The design almost certainly originated in the Johnstons mills at Newmill and is well over one hundred and twenty years old. The original design was much redder in tone but the estate now uses two versions – one heavier weight for the outdoors and the other lighter for both inside and outside use. Both are supplied by Glenlyon Tweed Mill. An updated version is planned to reflect the wider use of the tweed.

BALMORAL TWEEED

BALMORAL TARTAN

Balmoral

Balmoral lies on the Dee and is the property of Her Majesty The Queen. Prince Albert designed the Balmoral tartan sometime between 1848 and 1852 and the colouring of the tweed is the same. In Johnstons' records there is an entry showing that 'Super Balmoral tweed' was woven on 13 July 1853 but there is no record of the colouring. Clearly the tweed is a development of the tartan. There were frequent invoices from Johnstons to Macdougalls of Inverness in the 1850s for Balmoral tweed which makes one think that they sold it as a standard tweed, although nowadays its use is strictly confined to the Royal Estate. The ground is very dark navy and white giving a mid-grey cast with a sprinkling of red spots. HM The Queen kindly gave us permission to show the Balmoral tweed, tartan and Glenurquhart in our book.

BALMORAL LOVAT GLENURQUHART (HISTORICAL)

BALMORAL GLENURQUHART

Balmoral Lovat Glenurquhart (historical)

This is a true Glenurquhart in construction of very slight contrast. It is checked with one thread of crimson in the middle of the 2 and 2 part. The Balmoral Lovat Glenurquhart was formerly made by Blenkhorn Richardson & Co of Hawick. The Balmoral tweeds and tartan are not to be reproduced, being strictly confined to the Royal Family.

Balmoral Glenurquhart

This tweed is derived from the historical Glenurquhart (above) and is worn exclusively by the Royal Family.

Balnakeilly

The estate is near Moulin a little to the east of Pitlochry in Perthshire and was owned by Mr Aubyn JO Stewart-Wilson, the 12th Laird of Balnakeilly. The estate was sold in December 2016.

Mrs Grenville Stewart-Stevens, 10th Lady of Balnakeilly, designed the tweed when she succeeded her uncle Alexander Blair Stewart of Balnakeilly in 1936. This is a true Glenurquhart, the lighter colour a fawn paired with a dark reseda-green. There is an overcheck of two threads of soft blue on each side of the 4 x 4 part. The design was once most improperly pirated and was seen being worn by a member of parliament at lunch in The Savoy Grill. The laird hoped that this would never happen again.

Bateson (historical)

This is a tweed for which there are few facts. When my late grandfather-in-law produced his original book, he attributed the pattern to the west of Sutherland near Shieldaig. I have been unable to add any more information through my research but the design is old based on the invoice to MacDougalls of Inverness dated 27 July 1860. It seems reasonable to suppose that it was originally woven for an estate. While there is no definite proof that Johnstons created the original design this seems likely as the ing drab used for the Bateson was one of their special colours.

Ben Alder and Dalwhinnie

The estate lies at the summit of the
Drumochter Pass in Inverness-shire
and is owned by Ben Alder Estate Ltd.
Haggart's of Aberfeldy designed the tweed
for Mr PH Byam-Cook, a previous owner,
and it was introduced to the estate in 1967.

Ben More Assynt

The Ben More estate is at the top of the
River Oyke about thirty miles south-east
of Lochinver, the fishing town on the west
coast. The Vestey family trusts bought the
estate from the Godman family in 1982.
Hunters of Brora designed the tweed
and the Vestey family introduced it
in 1990. It is unusual because it has
a complicated system of overchecking
with a relatively small repeat of only eight
centimetres. Johnstons of Elgin introduced
the new tweed (shown here) in 2006.

BEN LOYAL

BEN LOYAL (ORIGINAL DESIGN)

Ben Loyal and Ben Loyal (original design)

Ben Loyal, owned by Anders Holch Povlsen, is located in the north of Sutherland, thirty miles from Lairg. It was originally part of the Sutherland estates but was one of ten estates sold in 1914. In 1939, Col Douglas Moncrieff purchased Loyal, who owned it until 1989, when Count Knuth bought it. The Count and Countess designed the original tweed with head stalker Ian Smart but in 1994 they changed it to a second design. The original is a little unusual as it has a herringbone ground with a double overcheck but the tweed currently in use is a Shepherd Check derivative with a quiet overcheck.

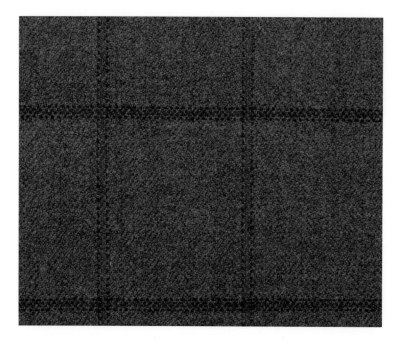

Black Corries

Black Corries in Glencoe, west of Rannoch Moor, is owned by the De Spoelberch family. Lord Pearson of Rannoch was the previous owner. The late Count Adolphe de Spoelberch designed the tweed and John Buchan of Waverly Mill, Galashiels was the supplier.

Ben Loyal Estate

Bolfracks

Bolfracks lies to the west of Aberfeldy on the south bank of the River Tay. Mr RA Price inherited the estate from his uncle Mr JD Hutchison in 1985. It was originally the home beat of the Taymouth estate and was bought by Mr Price's grandfather. Mr Hutchison designed the tweed with Haggart's of Aberfeldy in about 1960.

Boreland

Boreland is in Glen Lochay, Killin. The River Lochay runs into the southern end of Loch Tay, five miles south-west of Aberfeldy. Mr Mark Stroyan owns the tweed, which was designed by Ronald Stroyan in 1945 and was woven by Haggart's of Aberfeldy, now Glenlyon Tweed Mill.

Braeroy

Situated in Lochaber at Roybridge near Spean Bridge, Braeroy extends to more than 23,500 acres, rising from an altitude of 650 feet to 3,700 feet on the summit of Creag Meagaidh. Braeroy Ltd owns the tweed and it was woven by Haggarts of Aberfeldy, now Glenlyon Tweed Mill.

Braulen

Braulen estate lies in Glen Strathfarrar about twelve miles south-west from Inverness. Andras Limited owns it and Highland Adventures & Promotions Ltd now runs it, Estate Factors being Bidwells, Inverness. Braulen originally formed part of the Lovat estates and its current owners purchased it in 1990. Haggart's designed the new tweed while Glen Lyon Tweed Mill were commissioned to weave the exclusive tweed which will, in future, be worn by the stalkers and ghillies on Braulen estate. The image shown is the previous tweed.

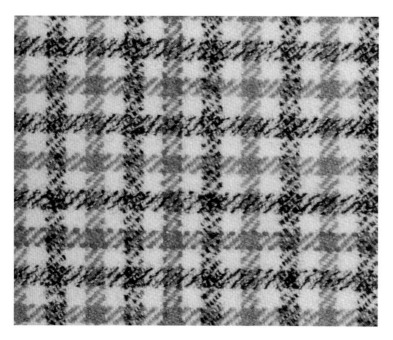

The Brook (historical)

This is one of the oldest patterns on Johnstons' list but it has no traceable history. I have included it in the hope that a reader may be able to shed some light on its origin.

The design is placed in the middle of a group of estate tweeds in an old Johnstons pattern book from the 1870s which would indicate that it belonged to an estate. It bears a startling resemblance to the Mamore, both in colour and in the unusual arrangement of the single red threads of the overchecking. The Kintail is another similar design which uses the single red thread to outline the overcheck.

Camusrory

The estate lies at the head of sea loch, Loch Nevis, which is fourteen miles or so east of Mallaig. The late colonel Sir Oliver Crosthwaite-Eyre designed the tweed in 1952 and it was originally used on the Knoydart estate of which Camusrory formed a part. It was reintroduced to Camusrory in 1993 when the Crosthwaite-Eyre family bought the estate from Mr R Wadsworth. Robert Crosthwaite Eyre and the Hon Rupert Soames now currently own the estate equally. Camusrory is reached by sea down Loch Nevis, the alternative being a ten-mile walk from Mallaig.

Candacraig

Candacraig estate lies in Donside about fifty miles west of Aberdeen and is owned by brothers George and Robert Wallace. Mr FA Wallace pioneered the tweed design in 1890, which was then altered slightly in 1950 by ALPF Wallace. As with all estate tweeds, the colours have differed a little over the years. The present version is much lighter in tone so that the twilled effect of the 1968 version is much less marked.

Cardrona (historical)

Cardrona estate is located in the Tweed valley five miles east of Peebles. It used to belong to Mr TD Ballantyne from Ballantynes of Walkerburn. He designed the tweed himself in 1947 and used it on the estate up to 1968 when he sold it. The tweed is now used by the Ballantyne family. The basic design is a gun club with a quiet overcheck. The repeat is about eight centimetres.

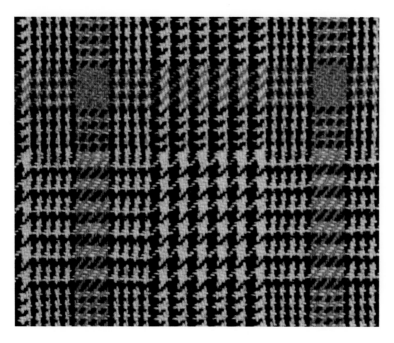

The Carnegie

The Carnegie is used on Southesk estate between Brechin and Montrose. Southesk Settlement, a Carnegie family trust, owns the estate, which is home to the Duke of Fife, head of the Carnegie family.

The design is a straightforward Glenurquhart but the handling of the overcheck is unusual. It is not known who designed the tweed but the first firm date is in a 1902 pattern book belonging to George Harrison of Edinburgh. It is believed that the tweed was introduced by the 9th Earl and the Earl of Northesk, another branch of the family, in about 1880. The great philanthropist Andrew Carnegie was photographed wearing the tweed in 1908.

Carnousie

The estate is situated along the Deveron river near Turriff in Aberdeenshire but there is no information about who designed the tweed or when it was introduced. It is a true Glenurquhart with the red guarding overcheck on the alternate basses of the 4 x 4 making a fairly large repeat of about fourteen centimetres. It is probably the darkest of the estate tweeds.

Cluanie and East Glenquoich

The estate is located on the south side of Glen Shiel facing the famous mountain range known as the five sisters of Kintail. Previous owner Christian Siva-Jothy sold the estate in 2016.

Cluanie is one of the oldest deer forests in Scotland. It was an exclusive royal forest as early as the 13th century. In 1509 the Laird of Grant received a charter from King James IV of Scotland appointing him forester. Lord Burton, one of the previous owners, entertained King Edward VII at Glen Quioch in 1904 and 1905. Mr Siva-Jothy bought the estate in 2003 and arranged for a new tweed to be designed. The current tweed is based on a number of local patterns and designed for its camouflage qualities.

Clune and Corrybrough

The estates of Clune and Corrybrough lie in the River Findhorn valley near the village of Tomatin. They are owned by His Grace, the Duke of Bedford's estate, which owns estates, farms, forests and properties across the UK. The current tweed design was developed having close regards to an older tweed. This was instructed by His Grace in 2013 and woven by Glenlyon Tweed Mill.

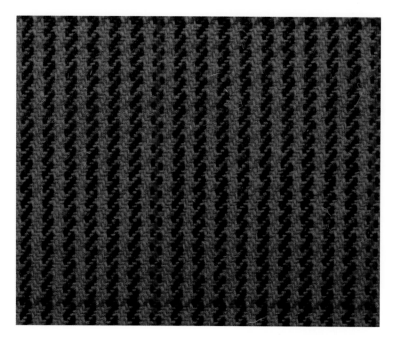

Craiganour

The estate lies on Loch Rannoch and is owned by Viscount Wimborne. Col and Mrs Parker designed the tweed in the 1950s and it was supplied by Haggart's of Aberfeldy, now Glenlyon Tweed Mill. Previous owners include Cobbolds of brewing fame and the Ismays who owned the White Star Line, builders of the Titanic.

Creag Dubh

Creag Dubh estate lies just south-west of Newtonmore. The estate is owned by Mr and Mrs A MacPherson who commissioned Araminta Campbell to design the tweed in 2015. As a Shepherd Check it is slightly unusual as it uses five base colours, creating a soft base to fit the varied colours of the Creag Dubh landscape.

Castle Fraser (historical)

Castle Fraser used to be owned by Major Michael Smiley. Mrs M Smiley adopted this simple Lovat with a double check of gold-brown twist in 1947. It was supplied by Russells of Insch in Aberdeenshire. Castle Fraser is one of the finest in Scotland and is part of the Castle Trail in Aberdeenshire. It is three miles from Monymusk and its previous name was the Castle of Muchal-in-Mar. It is unlikely that the tweed is still used on the estate as the castle is now property of the National Trust.

Cawdor

Cawdor estate and its castle of Macbeth fame lies inland about six miles south-west of Nairn on the Moray Firth. The castle is owned by the dowager Countess of Cawdor, whose husband, the 6th Earl of Cawdor, designed and introduced the tweed in 1980. It is still used on the estate. The pattern is a slightly unusual variant of the gun club as the red crossing of the weft is not repeated in the warp. The tweed is now made by Johnstons of Elgin.

Coigach (historical)

The estate and area of Coigach lie just north-west of Ullapool on the west coast. It was part of the lands of the Earls of Cromartie until 1950 when it was sold to the Henman and Longstaff families. The Coigach Salmon Fishings were sold separately.

There is no information on who designed the tweed nor even whether it was used on the estate but it seems likely. Johnstons first invoiced the tweed to MacDougalls of Inverness on 3 November 1846 and went on to make it in much greater quantities than could be used by one estate. The Earl of Cromartie suggested that it might have been used on the Sutherland estates as there was a connection by marriage between the two families. It is one of the great seminal designs not only of the estate tweeds but of the whole textile trade. The design was adopted in about 1874 by one of the gun clubs in the United States although the exact club remains unknown. Perhaps because the original name is hard to pronounce the name gun club stuck and this class of tweed design is now known as a gun club across the world.

Ceannacroc

Ceannacroc lies at the east end of Loch Cluanie in Upper Glenmoriston some fifteen miles west of Fort Augustus. It is owned by Mr Martin Girvan. There is, unfortunately, no information on the origins of the tweed used on the estate. It is a slightly unusual variant of the Shepherd Check as it uses various light colours in the warp and weft, although they may at one time have been the same. A double system of overchecks makes an exceptionally long repeat of about twenty centimetres. Bonnie Prince Charlie is supposed to have lived in a cave in the Ceannacroc hills after the 1745 uprising.

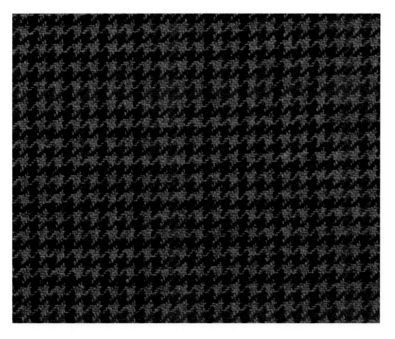

Conaglen

Conaglen estate was founded in 1858 when the Earl of Morton purchased the northern half of Ardgour as a sporting estate for deer stalking, fishing and grouse shooting from Alexander Maclean, the 14th Laird of Ardgour. Conaglen estate initially extended from the Glen Cona watershed in the south and was bordered to the east by Loch Linnhe and to the north by Loch Eil. Later the estate was extended after the purchase of Glafern from Sunart estate to border Loch Sheil in the west.

The Morton family introduced the estate tweed. It is understood that it was first designed by Hunters of Brora, who began trading in 1901. The tweed ceased being used on the estate sometime between the Second World War and 1959. The tweed was reintroduced in the late 1960s by the Guthrie family, who purchased the estate in 1959.

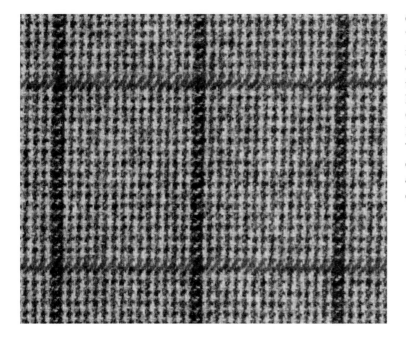

Cruach and Corrie Carie

The estate lies on Rannoch Moor some forty miles due west of Pitlochry and is owned by Lord Pearson of Rannoch and the Rannoch Trust. The estate used to be stalked from Black Corries Lodge in Glencoe but is now stalked from Rannoch Barracks at the west end of Loch Rannoch. The tweed in use, which was one of three differing grounds, was introduced in 1968 and was probably designed by Haggart's of Aberfeldy, now Glenlyon Tweed Mill.

Conaglen,
Fort William

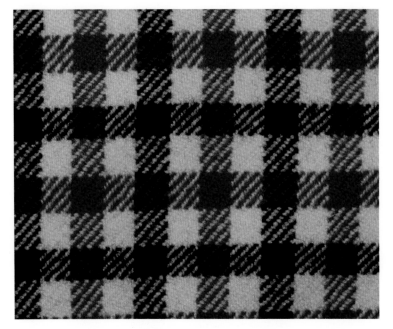

Dacre (historical)

This is one of the boldest of the estate checks and is simply the Coigach multiplied by two. Each check is three-eighths of an inch wide and while it would make a most conspicuous pattern walking down Princes Street in Edinburgh it would be fairly inconspicuous on the hill. As mentioned in 1968 there is no information on this tweed. Johnstons first invoiced it to Macdougalls of Inverness on 24 June, 1871 and it is likely that it was intended for some estate although the name is a curious one. In this respect it is like the Bateson. The Dacres were a well-known Border family and possibly the tweed is connected with them.

DALHOUSIE

DALHOUSIE INVERMARK

Dalhousie (used at Invermark) and Dalhousie (original design)

The estates of the Earl of Dalhousie lie ten miles north-west of Montrose. The estate of Invermark uses the tweed. There are two illustrations of the Dalhousie, the original from the 1968 book and the one in use at the present, showing how, over the years, a change or changes of maker can affect the appearance of the design. The weft check is almost invisible in the new version. The warp repeat, which does not show in the illustration, is about eleven centimetres. The ground design of a broken herringbone is most unusual.

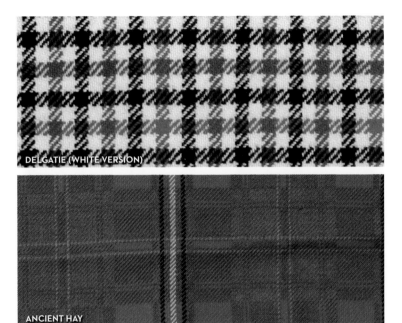

DELGATIE (WHITE VERSION)

ANCIENT HAY

Delgatie (brown version) and Delgatie (white version)

Delgatie Castle and estate are just beside Turriff. The late Captain John Hay of Delgatie transferred the castle and estate to the Delgatie Castle Trust over twenty years ago. The estate now uses the ancient Hay tartan but may use the Dupplin or Delgatie (white version) in the future. The white Delgatie shown here is a gun club with a red overcheck.

Dell

Dell Estate is on Loch Ness near Whitebridge. It has been owned since 2005 by Jeremy and Diana Finnis. Woven by Johnstons of Elgin, the tweed was designed by Mr and Mrs Finnis. They based the design on an older tweed. The main change was to replace a green line with a subtle purple one to represent the abundant heather on Dell Estate. The estate was previously owned by Lady Serena Bridgeman, daughter of the Earl of Bradford.

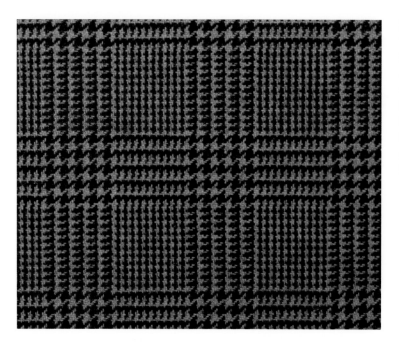

Dinnet

The estate lies between Aboyne and Ballater to the north of the River Dee. It is owned by Mr ECM Humphrey. The tweed was designed and introduced between the wars by Mr A Duley Hamilton. It is a fairly small Glenurquhart but the repeat is every twelve centimetres because the overchecking is on every alternate block of the 4 and 4.

Dorback

The estate is close to Grantown-on-Spey. It is owned by the Rebilly family. The tweed was designed by Lady Pauline Ogilvie-Grant Nicholson, a previous owner, in the 1970s. The estate was previously a Seafield estate and sold to the Rebilly family in 2000. The design is a Shepherd Check with overcheck. The ground check is varied by a slight difference in the depth of the dark colour in warp and weft. The tweed is woven by Glenlyon Tweed Mill.

Dinnet Estate

Dougarie

Dougarie is on the west coast of the Isle of Arran and belongs to Mr SC Gibbs. The estate was bought by Mr Gibbs from Lady Mary Boscawen in 1972. Originally as far back as the 1500s Dougarie belonged to the Dukes of Hamilton. It was inherited by the Duchess of Montrose and passed to Lady Mary. The present tweed was designed by Haggart's of Aberfeldy and is now woven by Glenlyon Tweed Mill. It was introduced by Mr Gibbs in 1974.

Derculich

An estate in Strathtay, near Aberfeldy, Perthshire. Originally part of Atholl, owners have included the Dempsters, sugar refiners in Gourock, the Nairn family, who made linoleum in Kirkcaldy, and the Honeyman family, who were linen manufacturers. More than forty years ago, the Jackson family from Lincolnshire bought the estate. The design is by William Jackson, the current owner, and Glenlyon Tweed Mill. Based on a local design, a band of Lincoln green has been added to represent the county of Jackson's birth. Derculich also has a series of tweeds, each telling the story of a connection to the family.

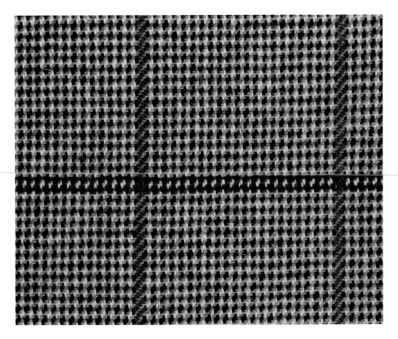

Drummond

The estate lies some six miles north of Auchterarder and belongs to Baroness Willoughby de Eresby. The purple warp check is a little unusual as is the effect of the light spot on the 2 and 2 in the centre of the crimson weft check. There is a thought that the purple dye was unusual and estate lore has it that it may have been sourced from Hungary. There is no information on who designed the tweed, which was in use in the 1880s and possibly earlier. It is known as the Glenartney Tweed. It is worn by the stalkers and keepers on the hill area of the Drummond Estate, which is centred in the medieval forest of Glenartney. The estate dates back to 1490 when John, First Lord Drummond, Steward of Strathearn and Justice General of Scotland was granted permission by James IV to build a stronghold on the edge of the rocky outcrop on which Drummond Castle now stands. At this time the Drummonds were already an old and distinguished Scottish family who continued to achieve positions of power and influence over the next five centuries. During Queen Victoria's visit in 1842, Prince Albert shot his first stag in Glenartney. Drummond Castle is located between Crieff and Muthill with the rest of the estate and Glenartney stretching towards the west. The tweed is woven by Glenlyon Tweed Mill.

Dunbeath

The Dunbeath and Grutt estate lies about twenty-four miles south of Wick and belongs to SW Murray Threapland. In previous times the estate formed part of the Sinclair lands and in 1650, as part of his campaign to put down the Covenanters, James Graham, Marquis of Montrose besieged Dunbeath Castle. The tweed was designed by Hunters of Brora and introduced in 1985 by Mr Avery, the previous owner of the estate.

Dunlossit

The estate is on the north-east coast of Islay running south for about ten miles from Port Askaig. The estate covers more than 18,500 acres of hill, woodland and farmland. The estate has been owned by the Schroder family since 1937 and it is thought that the design was introduced in the 1920s. At that time the Islay Woollen Mills were let to Mr JT Christie and it is assumed that he was the designer. It is a simple pattern with a fairly bold red overcheck and a very quiet blue one which tends to sink into the ground colouring.

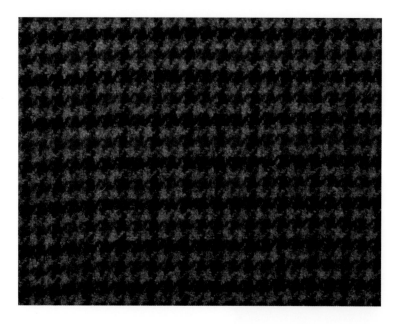

Dunecht

Dunecht Estates are owned by the Hon Charles Pearson. The estates comprise six separate estates in Aberdeenshire and Kincardineshire, namely: Dunecht, Raemoir, Forest of Birse, Dunnottar Castle, West Durris and Edinglassie. The pattern is a straightforward gun club and was introduced to the estate by Annie, 1st Viscountess Cowdray in February 1927. It seems probable that she was the designer. The tweed is sometimes called The Cowdray.

Dungarthill

The estate is three miles from Dunkeld, Perthshire and has been owned by Mr and Mrs CJ Hoogstede since 1992. The original tweed was designed jointly by Haggart's of Aberfeldy and Neil Hoogstede Conlier. This had red as the estate colour and orange as the Dutch influence. The sample is a subsequent 'lighter' tweed from Glenlyon Tweed Mill with a slight alteration to the design.

Edradynate

The estate is on the north bank of the River Tay about three miles north-east of Aberfeldy. It is the property of the family of Michael DCC Campbell MBE DL who bought it from Major David Gibson in 1983. Before that Edradynate had belonged to the Stewarts, Stewart-Robertsons and Stewart Meiklejohns for five hundred years from 1485. Mr Campbell introduced the tweed to the estate with Haggart's of Aberfeldy in 1983. The quiet chrome-coloured stripe between the red stripes tends to sink into the ground colour. The bold red stripes represent Breadalbane. Mr Campbell is a Loudoun Campbell and the Loudouns are a sept of the Breadalbanes.

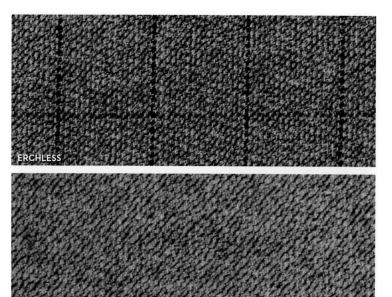

ERCHLESS

ERCHLESS (ORIGINAL)

Erchless and Erchless (original design)

Castle Erchless is on the River Beauly to the west of Inverness and the estate covers a great area of mountainous country. It was originally a Chisholm estate and was sold to Baron Stackelberg in 1946 and then to Sir Lawrence Robson in 1964. The original tweed had no overchecking and was slightly yellower in tone than the present. It was presumably designed by the Chisholms as Johnstons invoiced it to Macdougalls of Inverness in August 1852. There is no information on who designed the present tweed but it is like the Gannochy and Glencanisp (designed by Hunters of Brora), the difference lying in the colour of the overcheck.

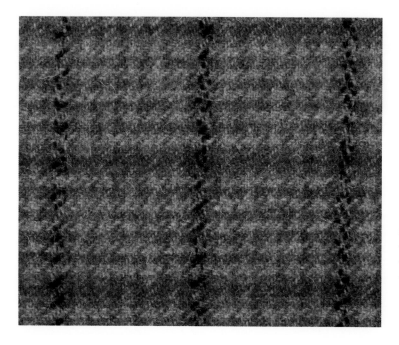

Eilanreach

Eilanreach lies on the Sound of Sleat on the mainland just opposite the Isle of Skye near Glenelg. It is owned by the Trustees of Eilanreach Estate. The tweed was designed in around 1950 by the then owners Lord and Lady Dulverton and Sir John MacLeod who owned the Cuchulin Handloom Company. Originally the estate was owned by the Baillies of Dochfour and was rented for a number of years at the turn of the century by the Master of Blantyre. The estate was then sold to the Scott family from the Hill of Nigg who in turn sold it to the Dulvertons in 1947. The tweed is unusual in having a bold black and yellow twist for its warp overcheck element.

Esslemont

Esslemont lies slightly west of Ellon and fifteen miles north of Aberdeen and is owned by Charles Iain Wolrige Gordon of Esslemont. It has been in the family since 1720. Before 1720 the family seat was at Hallhead adjoining Craigievar but when the Laird went bankrupt he was bought out by his younger brother who had made a fortune in claret in Bordeaux. At the same time he bought Esslemont. He and his eldest son were ardent Jacobites, the latter being greatly involved in the '45 rebellion. After the '45 he went into exile in France where he died and the estates were forfeited to the Crown. The estates were returned to the family in 1760 when the eldest son returned from France. The tweed was designed by Charles Iain Robert Wolrige Gordon of Esslemont and his wife. It was introduced in 1960. Woven by Glenlyon Tweed Mill.

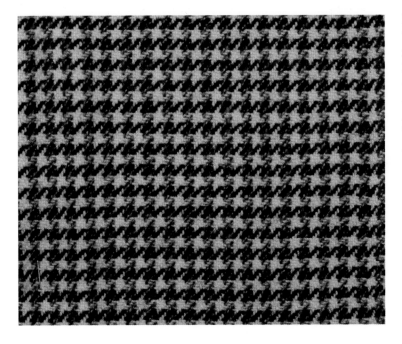

Fairburn

The estate is five miles west of Muir of Ord in Ross-shire. It is owned by Mrs Charlotte Kythe Hingston of Fairburn and the tweed was introduced in about 1925 by Major Sir John Stirling, KT, MBE. It was designed by A & J Macnab of Slateford near Edinburgh. The Stirling family have owned Fairburn since the 1870s and continue to do so.

Fannich

Fannich lies to the east of Loch Maree in Ross and Cromarty, about twenty miles south of Ullapool. It belongs to Fannich Estate Ltd. Vernon Watney bought the estate in 1900 and is said to have introduced the tweed but Johnstons invoiced it to Macdougalls of Inverness as far back as 3 July 1860. There is, however, no evidence to show who designed it and Johnstons may not even have been the first makers. The estate was subsequently sold to Mr TW Sandeman, who sold it to Baron W van Dedem in 1976, who then sold it to Fannich Estate Ltd.

Farleyer

The estate lies just five miles east of Aberfeldy in Perthshire and belongs to Iain Wotherspoon who acquired it in 2003. Since 2016 Mr Wotherspoon has leased the estate and continues to retain stalking rights and rights to the tweed, which is woven by Glenlyon Tweed Mill. Fortingall Hotel (which used to form part of the estate) was refurbished by the Wotherspoons in 2006 and features ten local tweeds, including Farleyer. The estate originally belonged to Major NG Ramsay who designed and introduced the tweed in 1955 as the maker of the previous tweed had gone out of business. The estate, less the original house and policies, was bought by the Fane family in 1988 together with the right to wear the tweed, which is still in use on the estate. The estate house is now the Manse at Weem near Aberfeldy.

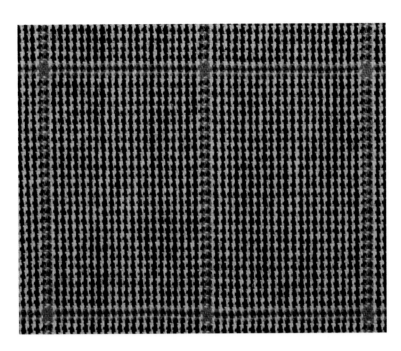

Farr

Farr lies twelve miles to the south of Inverness and belongs to Philip Mackenzie. The estate has been in the Mackenzie family for more than 140 years. It is believed that the tweed was probably introduced to the estate by the late Austin Mackenzie of Carradale in around 1900 and he may well have designed it. The tweed is woven by Glenlyon Tweed Mill.

Fassfern

The estate is owned by West Highland Woodlands and is situated ten miles west of Fort William. The estate extends to 17,000 acres of deer forest and 9,000 acres of forestry. Over the years, the estate was bought from Achnacarry, primarily for forestry, with the deer forest purchased in 1999. The tweed was designed by the family in 2001.

Fasnacloich

The estate is owned by David Stewart and is at Appin, North Argyll. Apart from the period 1901 to 1992 the estate has been in Appin Stewart ownership since the 14th century. The tweed was designed in 1994 by Hunters of Brora and Mr and Mrs Stewart.

Findynate

Located in Strathtay, Perthshire, the estate has been owned by members of the Stewart clan and by Viscountess Ridley. Upon her death in 2007, the estate was purchased by Reggeborgh Group Ltd. The tweed was designed in 2008 by the family who own the Reggeborgh Group in conjunction with the weavers, Glenlyon Tweed Mill. The tweed was designed to include several colours representing the area in the Netherlands, the original home of the owners.

Flichity

The estate is owned by Tim and Sarah Leslie and is situated near Farr, Inverness-shire. The tweed was designed by Tim Leslie in 2009.

Finzean

The estate lies in the Feugh Valley near Aboyne and has been owned by the Farquharsons of Finzean for sixteen generations since 1609, the current owners being Donald and Andrew of that ilk. The grouse moor on the estate was first let in 1840. The estate tweed was introduced by the family in 1964 and the design was a modification of a tweed created by Mr Tom Simpson of Hunters of Brora. The repeat is fairly large, about twelve centimetres, and the gold lines are a stripe, not repeated in the weft.

Ford and
Etal Estate

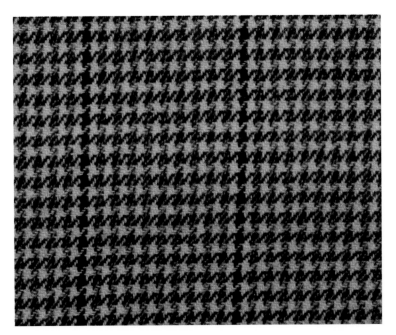

Ford and Etal

The estate is ten miles south-south-west of Berwick and is owned by the 5th Lord Joicey. Strictly speaking it is an English estate but while not really part of what were known as the Debatable Lands, owing to the south-westerly direction of the Border, it is only three miles from it. The name of the designer is not known but the tweed was introduced by the 1st Lord Joicey in about 1920. The Scottish connection is underlined as the tweed was made by Haggart's of Aberfeldy, now Glenlyon Tweed Mill. As a checked Shepherd it is slightly unusual as the weft checking is lighter than the ground and therefore the warp check has a striped effect.

Fyvie

The estate is near Turriff in Aberdeenshire and while the castle is now the property of the National Trust for Scotland, the estate is owned by Sir George I D Forbes-Leith Bt. The tweed was certainly introduced as far back as 1889, possibly earlier, but there is no evidence of who designed it. As protective colouring in the area it is ideal.

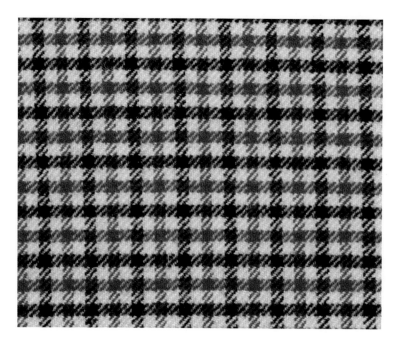

Gairloch (historical)

This pattern comes from the area of Gairloch in Wester Ross and its claim to a place in this book may be a little doubtful. Johnstons first invoiced the pattern to Macdougalls of Inverness on 15 July, 1846 and it seems reasonable to suppose that it was for the Gairloch estate. It is almost an exact copy of the Coigach: the dark colours are identical, but in the weft the white ground is replaced with a yellow and white twist. This slight alteration gives a much warmer effect to the pattern as a whole.

Gannochy

The estate is in Glen Esk, Angus, about ten miles north of Brechin. It dates back to the 12th century when it was owned by the Stirling family. By the 18th century it was part of the large Dalhousie Estates. Royalty were regular visitors to Glen Esk, including the future Queen Elizabeth with her father King George VI. In the 1960s Dalhousie sold Gannochy to William Foster, who sold it in the 1980s to an American, Derald Ruttenberg. He sold to Edinmore Properties who then sold to Mr Hemmings. By the turn of the century the estate properties were in a poor state of repair. In 2003, the estate was broken down into smaller lots. Enormous energy, a modern approach and focused investment resulted in a rebirth of Glen Esk with thriving wildlife and a stronger local economy. Gannochy has, since 2004, a reputation for guests achieving a Macnab. This is to shoot a brace of grouse, catch a salmon and stalk and shoot a stag, all in the same day. See Pitgaveny for the history of a Macnab. The original tweed was designed in 1983 by the owners at that time, Mr and Mrs DH Ruttenberg. A new design (pictured) was introduced by Mr Hemmings and Dave Clement.

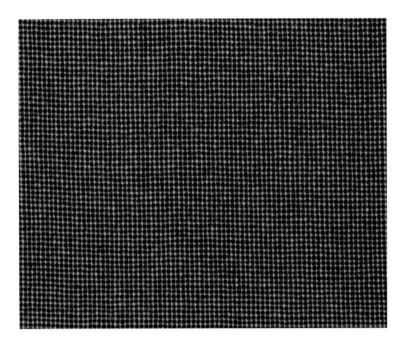

Garden

Garden is owned by Archibald Stirling and has been in the Stirling family since the beginning of the 17th century. Garden Estate is in West Stirlingshire near Buchlyvie. In around 1920 the tweed was designed by Colonel Archibald Stirling of Garden and Sir John Stirling-Maxwell of Pollock and Corrour to be a derivative of the Corrour. The Garden tweed is unique amongst Scottish estate tweeds in being more like an Irish Donegal than a Scottish cloth. It is what is known in the weaving trade as a 'plain cloth' with one thread of black and one of white in the warp being crossed with a tawny yellow in the weft. It is in regular use.

Glenample

Glenample is at the western end of Loch Earn on the south side, thirty miles west of Perth. The estate is owned by Maria Jose lleo, widow of Rafael Cruz-Conde. He bought the estate in 1992 from Mr D Abbot who had purchased it in 1988 from the Stirlings of Keir. They had bought the estate from the Waters McRae of Edinample. Senor Cruz-Conde designed the tweed with Haggart's of Aberfeldy and introduced it in 1994. The tweed is in regular use.

Glenavon

Glenavon is in the Cairngorms, twenty miles or so east of Aviemore. It is owned by Andras Ltd, who bought it in 1995 from the Seaton Wills family, and is now run by Highland Adventures & Promotions Ltd, estate factors being Bidwells, Inverness. Before 1995 the estate belonged to the Duke of Richmond and Gordon who sold it to Colonel Oliver Haigh. The new tweed was designed by Haggart's of Aberfeldy and the estate owners. Glenlyon Tweed Mill was commissioned to weave the exclusive tweed, which is now worn by Glenavon estate keepers.

North Glenbuchat

The estates of North and South Glenbuchat are in Strathdon, Aberdeenshire where the Water of Buchat joins the River Don. Until 1969 they were one estate, bought by Mr James W Barclay in 1901. The northern part was sold to Lord Cowdray and the Hon Mrs Lavinia Smiley in 1969 and sold again to Mr DWF Tulloch in 1981. It is now owned by the family of Lord Milford Haven. Mrs Barclay Sole, granddaughter of Mr James Barclay, and her son retained the southern part. The estate tweeds were commissioned by Mrs Sole's father and the only difference in them is the colour of the overcheck. An excellent local history, *The Book of Glenbuchat*, was published in 1942.

South Glenbuchat

The estate neighbours of North Glenbuchat. The Barclay Sole family bought Glenbuchat Estate in 1901. With North Glenbuchat sold in 1969, South Glenbuchat was created, owned by the Barclay Sole family. In 2013, the estate was split into three. Peter and Lesley Robinson own what is known as South Glenbuchat.

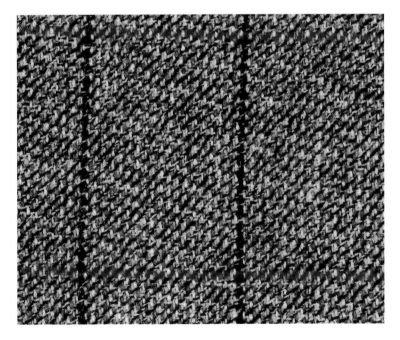

Glencanisp (historical)

The estate lies just to the east of Lochinver on the west coast. It was once part of the Sutherland Estates but has been owned by the Vestey family who sold it to Assynt Foundation in 2005. The tweed is not in current use so we show it for historical purposes. The design, like the Ben More Assynt tweed, is by Hunters of Brora and was introduced by the Vestey family in 1990. The tweed is like the Gannochy and the Erchless, the differences lying in the overchecking colouring.

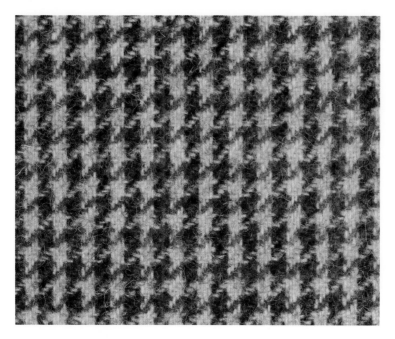

Glendelvine and Riemore

This attractive and quiet tweed is used on two estates, Glendelvine and Riemore, in the Dunkeld district of Perthshire. Both estates have belonged to the Lyle family for generations, owned by Sir Gavin Lyle, Bt (Glendelvine) and Baroness Linklater of Butterstone (Riemore) who has now sold to the Riemore Trust. The tweed pattern was introduced by Sir Alexander Lyle, Bt in about 1920 and was made by Hunters of Brora. It is a simple Shepherd Check in browns with a very quiet overcheck. The Glendelvine stretch of the River Tay has some excellent fly water and is rated as the best. It is where Miss Georgina Ballantyne caught her record 64lb salmon in 1922. The fish remains the largest salmon caught on rod and line in the British Isles to this day.

Glen Dessary

The estate is situated between Loch Nevis and Loch Arkaig, 30 miles west of Fort William. It is owned by Sir Patrick Grant of Dalvey Bt. The estate is in Knoydart, a mountainous area next to Loch Nevis and covers 15,000 acres. Bonnie Prince Charlie hid there twice. The tweed was designed by Ronald Schmitt in 1980 and is in regular use.

GLENDOE

GLENDOE (ORIGINAL DESIGN)

Glendoe and Glendoe (original design)

Glendoe lies on the south side of Loch Ness near Fort Augustus and belongs to the Vernon family through Hillhouse Estates Limited. There are two estate tweeds. The first is the one in use at present, designed by Hunters of Brora and introduced by the Vernons in 1993. The second pattern was given to my grandfather in law by Campbell's of Beauly in 1967 but there was no information on where the tweed came from or who designed it. In the 1870s Glendoe was part of the Lovat lands and was sold to Philip Noble of Ponteland, Newcastle in 1919. It was subsequently owned for many years after the second world war by Olaf Hambro of the banking family, and for a number of years by Admiral William Beveridge Mackenzie. The tweed is in regular use.

Glen Dye

Glen Dye is to the west of Aberdeenshire. At present the estate is owned by Mr Charles Gladstone and it has been in his family for almost 200 years. It was acquired by John Gladstone who became 1st Baronet of Pasque and Balfour. His son William became prime minister during Queen Victoria's reign. The Glen Dye estate was added in the 1840s. There is no information on exactly when the tweed was introduced but the Gladstone family probably designed it.

Glenfeshie

Glenfeshie lies ten miles or so south of
Aviemore. It was owned by the Duke of
Gordon until 1812 then the Macphersons
of Ballindalloch until 1967. Lord Dulverton
owned it until 1986 and sold to Mr Dibden.
In 1993 he sold to Wills Woodland Trust.
They sold to Klaus Helmerson in 1998 who
then sold to Flemming Skouboe in 2001.
He then sold to Anders Holch Povlsen.

Glenfeshie works to protect and
preserve its wild nature and beauty.
Through its wildlife company, Glenfeshie
is also working to preserve and regenerate
vast areas across Scotland.

Lord Dulverton introduced the tweed
when he took over the estate in 1967 but
the designer is not known. The pattern is
a simple Shepherd Check with an unusual
marled overcheck. The original Glenfeshie
tweed, designed by Miss Balfour, can be
seen under Aberchalder (page 32).

Glenfinnan

Glenfinnan is at the head of Loch Shiel, west of Fort William, where the monument commemorates the gathering of the clans at the start of the 1745 rebellion. The estate is owned by Ian Leith. The design was introduced by Macdonald of Glenalladale sometime between 1910 and 1930. The previous owner, Mr MR Warren, made slight changes. The land around Glenfinnan is unusually sandy coloured and bright and the tweed blends in admirably on the hill.

Glenisla

The estate lies beside Cortachy, a village about eight miles north-west of Forfar, and is the property of the Airlie Estates Heritage Trust. There is no definite information on who designed the tweed but Lord Airlie thinks it may have been his great-grandmother Blanche, Countess of Airlie, who introduced it to the estate in about 1880. It has been used on the estate ever since. The design is a Glenurquhart in brown and white, differing in size from the true Glenurquhart and, except for the colour, similar to the Green Mar. The tweed is also used on Glenisla and the larger Airlie Estates.

Glenlyon

The estate lies three miles north of Loch Tay. It is owned by Mr and Mrs Iain Wotherspoon who acquired it in 2002 from Mr and Mrs Lars Foghsgaard. They had acquired it from the descendants of the late Sir Donald Currie who had taken over Glenlyon and the surrounding estates of North Chesthill and Garth in 1885. The tweed is woven by Glenlyon Tweed Mill.

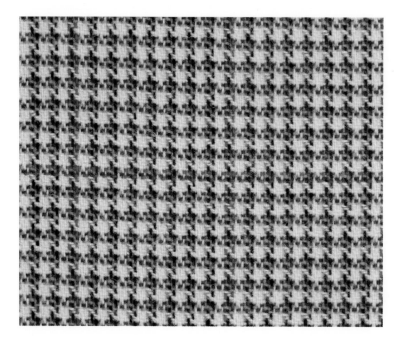

Glenmoidart (historical)

Glenmoidart lies on the west of Loch Shiel, twenty miles from Fort William. It is owned by the Trustees of Glenmoidart Estate. There is no evidence on when the tweed was introduced to the estate or who designed it. The design is unusual in that the ground weave is a small diamond and not the usual twill. The tweed was seldom used on the hill as it was too light.

Glen Moriston (historical)

As the crow flies Glen Moriston is five miles north-west of Fort Augustus. The glen starts at Invermoriston on Loch Ness and the estate belonged to the Grant family for nearly six hundred years. In the late 1980s part of the estate was sold off and fragmented but a portion and the house were retained by the Grants. The tweed is one of the oldest estate tweeds there is and first appears in the Johnstons sales book on 22 July 1851. It may have been adopted by Caroline, Countess of Seafield as her estate of Glenurquhart lies immediately to the east. The design was extensively adopted by the tweed trade in the late 19th century. It was found to be too bright for use on the hill and it was replaced in the 20th century by stock tweeds from Campbell's of Beauly.

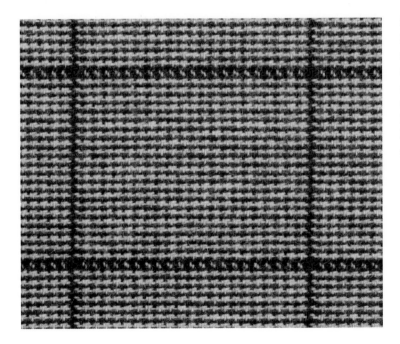

Glenmuick

Glenmuick is just south of the River Dee at Ballater. The tweed was introduced to the estate by the Mackenzie family who owned it in the 19th century. Its use was continued by the Walker-Okeover family who bought the estate from the Mackenzies in 1948. The estate is now owned by Sir Andrew Walker-Okeover.

Glen Orchy (historical)

Glen Orchy is in Argyllshire near Dalmally, about thirty miles south-east of Fort William. It once belonged to the Campbells of Breadalbane but was sold to Sir Douglas Montgomery Hall in 1936 and then to the late Captain Oldham in 1946. Forestry Commission Scotland bought the estate in 1967 when it became part of the National Forest Estate. The tweed has not been in use for around fifty years but it is unusually colourful and there may have been a Shepherd Check type in the same colours as the Glenurquhart version illustrated.

GLENOGIL

GLENOGIL (ORIGINAL DESIGN)

Glenogil (1970 design) and Glenogil (original design)

Glenogil lies about eight miles north of Forfar and between Glen Clova and Glen Lethnot in the famed Angus Glens. The Woolton Trustees bought the estate from Lord Woolton's stepfather, the late Lord Forres, in 1974 and continued to use the estate tweed. The original tweed was designed by Lord Forres and the Strathmore Woollen Company but in around 1970 this was replaced by another tweed designed by Hunters of Brora. The estate has reverted to using the original design.

Glenprosen

The estate is ten miles north of Kirriemuir and is owned by Robin Batchelor. It is a traditional Scottish estate stretching to 16,500 acres at the top of the glen. The tweed was designed by Glenlyon Tweed Mill in 2011 as an all-round estate tweed for use in deer stalking and grouse shooting, hence the brown base. The lines represent natural resource products: black for oil, yellow for gold and red for iron. Protection, preservation and careful management of natural resources is a priority at Glenprosen. The estate features the opportunity to compete for a 'Macnab'. This is stalk a stag, catch a salmon and shoot a brace of grouse, all in the same day (see Pitgaveny for the history of a Macnab). Successful 'Macnabbers' from around the world can attend the annual Field Macnab challenge dinner in London.

Glensanda (historical)

Glensanda lies on the Morvern Peninsula in North Argyll. Originally it formed part of the territory of the Macleans of Kingairloch but a gambling debt of £11,000, incurred in a London club in 1800, forced the family to sell to James Forbes of Hutton Hall, Essex, who owned the adjoining Kingairloch Estate. In 1902 Glensanda, along with Kingairloch, was bought by George Herbert Strutt of Belper, Derbyshire, great-great-grandson of Jedediah Strutt who was co-founder with Sir Richard Arkwright of the cotton spinning industry in Great Britain. Glensanda was sold by the Strutt family to Foster Yeoman Ltd, Shepton Mallet, Somerset, in 1982 and is now owned by Aggregate Industries plc. The Glensanda tweed was introduced in 1984 and is based on an old estate pattern.

Glenshero

In 1929 the British Aluminium Company completed its major hydro construction programme of dams and pipework to carry water to its new aluminium smelters at Fort William and Kinlochleven. When the company bought Glenshero Estate in 1932, further work was carried out to put in hydro power infrastructure, from within the estate's water catchment, which contains the headwaters of the River Spey. Today, the estate still carries out traditional sporting activities. Lying just to the west of the Monadhliath Mountains, it encompasses the Corrieyairack, Sherramore and Glenshirra deer forests. The estate also contains the historic 2,500-feet-high Corrieyairack Pass, which runs from Laggan to Fort Augustus and was completed by General Wade in 1732 from a former drovers' road. In the early 1980s, after Alcan acquired the estate, a tweed was commissioned and is worn today by the stalkers of Glenshero Estate.

GLEN TANAR ORIGINAL

GLEN TANAR LIGHTWEIGHT

Glen Tanar and Glen Tanar (lightweight pattern)

The estate lies four miles to the south-west of Aboyne on Deeside. The original pattern was probably introduced in around 1912 by the first Lord Glentanar and it has proved an effective camouflage on the hill. In 1995 Mrs Bruce sent a pattern of a lighter-weight worsted cloth which is also used on the estate. While the basic pattern remains the same, though smaller, the variation in depth of colour is dramatic. In 1905 the estate was bought by George Coats, later Lord Glentanar. It is now owned by Claire and Michael Bruce, the fourth generation to own and care for Glen Tanar. In 2015 they commissioned Araminta Campbell to modernise the tweed but still reflecting the forest and moorings of Glen Tanar and remaining true to the original. This is worn successfully by keepers so we have a fascinating example of evolution of a tweed. Woven by Glenlyon Tweed Mill.

GLEN TANAR (ARAMINTA)

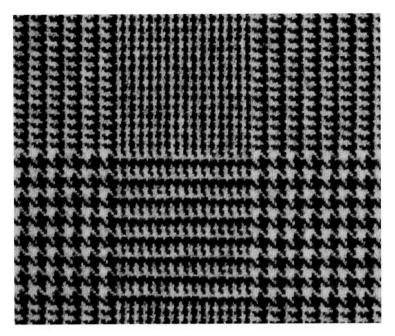

Glenurquhart (historical)

The Glenurquhart is one of a small list of outstanding designs that has influenced fashion houses all over the world. It was adapted by Caroline, Countess of Seafield for her estates in about 1840. The story has it that the design was created by Elizabeth Macdougall of Lewiston and is a combination of a portion of the Shepherd Check and another pattern woven two of black and two of white, approximately two inches each. The designer had great difficulty in getting William Fraser, the weaver, to understand her instructions and she sketched the pattern in the mud at the cottage door. The design was originally in dark blue and white but was later changed to the black and white that we see today. Interestingly enough in the Day Book of Johnstons for June 1851, there is an invoice for a web of Glenurquhart for Macdougalls of Inverness and in the same month a web of Coigach and a web of Glen Moriston for the same customer. Glen Moriston is the next glen to the west of Glenurquhart and was also part of the Seafield estates. This invoice suggests that the original pattern created early in the 1840s for Glenurquhart was originally woven commercially at the mill at Drumnadrochit and from there the manufacture moved to Inverness. It is not unreasonable to assume that it might have taken ten years to get from William Fraser's narrow loom in the west to the more sophisticated broadlooms of Johnstons. The Drumnadrochit mill closed down early in the 1950s and was then used as a house. The mill was one of the first attempts to introduce industry to the Highlands after the '45 and was built by the Laird of Grant at the same time as the Honourable Commissioners for the Annexed Estates built the mill at Invermoriston close by. The lists of the women to whom the King's Commissioners distributed spinning wheels to supply yarn to the mills can be found in the archives of Castle Grant.

Gordon Castle

The estate is on the outskirts of Fochabers, Moray and is owned by Angus and Zara Gordon Lennox. It is not known precisely when the Gordon Castle tweed was developed but it was widely used from the late 19th century on the vast Scottish sporting estates of the Dukes of Richmond and Gordon, which included Glenfiddich, Glenlivet, Kinrara and the fishing on the River Spey at Fochabers. Sold in the middle of the 20th century, some fishing on the Spey and the castle itself were repurchased by the Duke's grandson, Lieutenant General Sir George Gordon Lennox after the second

world war. The tweed had been in continuous use throughout and is still worn today by the ghillies on the River Spey and other employees at Gordon Castle.

The castle had a walled garden existing in the 17th century. The current walled garden was built in 1808. It covers eight acres and is thought to be the largest in Scotland. The Gordon Lennox family have been painstakingly restoring their ancestors' garden. The estate run eight miles of continuous fishing on the River Spey. Gordon Castle has been a Johnstons customer since the early 1800s.

Gordon Castle Ghillies in 1911 (above) and 2011 (below)

MARK WILLIAMSON

Gorrenberry

The estate is situated in Liddesdale, Roxburghshire on the Southern uplands. It is owned by Professor D Jane Bower who bought it in 2011. It was part of Buccleuch Estate until 1976. The tweed was designed by Johnstons of Elgin in 2011 and it is in regular use. The estate has farmland, steep hills, rivers and woodlands. One of these, covering 366 hectares, was replanted during the Diamond Jubilee of Her Majesty Queen Elizabeth II and is recorded as Jubilee Woods.

Guisachan

The old estate of Guisachan has been split into three smaller properties. It lies 30 miles west of Inverness at the head of Strathglass and was originally part of the lands of the Frasers, on the frontier of the Chisholms' land. In 1854 it was bought by Lord Tweedmouth who made extensive improvements to the lodge and village and entertained King George V there. It also lays claim to being the place where Sir Winston Churchill learned to drive and it is the birthplace of the Golden Retriever. The estate was broken up in the 1930s and Nigel Fraser owns the Home farm and low ground. The Guisachan tweed was first invoiced by Johnstons to Macdougalls of Inverness on 15 August 1861. It is used on the estate. The tweed is woven by Johnstons of Elgin.

Haddo

Haddo Estate lies 20 miles north-west of
Aberdeen. It is owned by the Marquess
of Aberdeen and Temair. The tweed
originates from the Guisachan Estate in
Glen Affric. The great-grandfather of the
Marquess married Ishbel Marjoribanks
in 1877 and her father, who was the first
Lord Tweedmouth, bought the Guisachan
Estate in around the 1850s. He had his
own estate tweed made, which was based
on a brown and yellow check, and this is
still in use. The Haddo Estate tweed was
modelled on this pattern but the brown
and yellow was changed to blue and
yellow to reflect the Gordon colours. It is
woven by Johnstons of Elgin.

Inge (historical)

The Inge probably originated in the Elgin mills of Johnstons of Elgin and the first record of it was in September 1846. There does not seem to have been an estate of this name and it is impossible to trace its antecedents. About that time Affric was leased to a Colonel Inge and one can only speculate that the pattern was used for his stalkers. However, it was made so frequently in the 1850s and 1860s that Macdougalls must have sold it to all and sundry. The unusual red-brown colour, known in the mill as the Ing Drab, occurs in other tweeds.

Innes

Innes House is one of the finest 17th century houses in Scotland and was built by Sir Robert Innes of that Ilk in 1640. The house is six miles east of Elgin in Morayshire. The house and estate were owned by Mark Tennant but he has now made them over to his son Edward. The original tweed was made as long ago as 1872 as there is a note from Christie & Son of Edinburgh to Johnstons of Elgin, dated 17 April asking for a delivery date. It was subsequently made by Hunters of Brora. At some time a new tweed was introduced and this is the one pictured. The keepers used to beat on grouse moors where they were known as 'the Green Army' as they could be seen for miles.

Invercauld

The estate of Invercauld lies on upper
Deeside, close to Balmoral, west and
south of Braemar, and belongs to the
Farquharson Family Trust. Captain
AAC Farquharson thinks the tweed
was probably introduced by his great-
grandfather Colonel James Ross
Farquharson in the late 1800s. Johnstons
of Elgin certainly made the pattern in
the 1870s as it appears in one of the old
pattern books. At that time the general
tone was much less brown and the green
overcheck much darker but there has
been no change in the basic pattern.

Wemyss and
March Estate

INVERAILORT

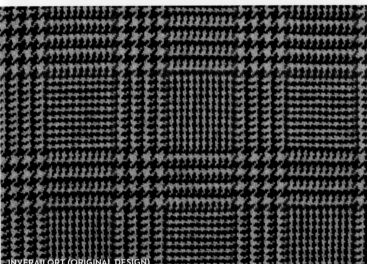

INVERAILORT (ORIGINAL DESIGN)

Inverailort and Inverailort (original design)

Inverailort Estate lies twenty-five miles west of Fort William on the Road to the Isles. During the second world war the estate was requisitioned by the War Office and became the First Special Training Centre in Scotland, occupied by the Commandos, the SOE and latterly the Navy.

The estate has receipts of supply of the original tweed in 1912 from JA Chisolm & Co of Holm Mill, Inverness. The second (new) tweed was designed by Hunters of Brora. Inverailort Estate now wears both tweeds.

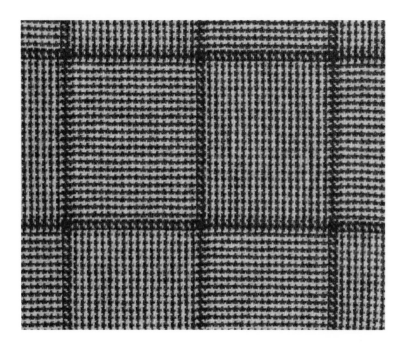

Inveraray (historical)
This is a handsome and simple design which has been on the books of Johnstons of Elgin for well over a hundred and forty years. The origin of the design is lost and, curiously enough, neither Mr Angus MacIntyre of the well-known tweed warehouse in Inveraray nor his father had any knowledge of the pattern when it was illustrated in the first edition of this book. Indeed Argyll Estates confirms that it does not have a special tweed of its own.

Inveraray (Glenkinglass design) (historical)
In the late 1940s Mr Michael Noble, later Lord Glenkinglass, gave this pattern to Mr MacIntyre as the Inveraray with the request that he get a length made up. Mr MacIntyre had it made by Alexanders of Peterhead from which this sample came but I have no information on its antecedents, nor has the estate.

Invermark (historical)

Invermark is one of the estates owned by the Earl of Dalhousie and lies west of Montrose in Glenesk). The estate now uses the Dalhousie tweed (see page 60) but formerly used this striking Glenurquhart with its two thread scarlet overcheck on the 2 and 2 section. The repeat, which is not very obvious in the illustration, is about nine centimetres. Nothing is known of the designer or when it was introduced but there is a possibility that it was once woven with a basket effect on the 2 and 2 section.

Islay

Islay Estates Company owns some 55,000 acres in central and north-east Islay. It is owned by the Morrison family whose head is Lord Margadale of Islay. It is believed that the tweed was introduced in the early 1900s and, as it was made at the local Islay Woollen Mill, it was probably designed by Mr JT Christie who had the lease of the mill at that time. Back in the 1850s most of the island was owned by James Morrison and the estate has belonged to the family ever since. The tweed is also used on the family estates in Wiltshire.

Jahama Highland Estates

The Gupta Family Group Alliance owns Liberty British Aluminium, the company that in December 2016 bought the Lochaber Aluminium Smelter and the surrounding estates, which provide the catchment area for the water supply to the hydro power stations at Fort William and Kinlochleven. These estates, now Jahama Highland Estates, are a collection of more than 114,000 acres located around Fort William, Kinlochleven and Laggan. The land is made up of some of the most stunning scenery in Europe and surrounds Ben Nevis, the UK's highest mountain. In summer 2017, Johnstons of Elgin was commissioned by the Gupta family to design and produce the Jahama Highland Estates tweed which is work in progress.

Kellas and Brokentore

This tweed was designed in 1982 for use by the Christie family and on Kellas Estate. Kellas and Brokentore are five miles south of Elgin. The tweed was designed by Colin Barclay (head keeper) and estate owner Tomas Christie. The plain layout background was chosen because of the Christie family connection to the Lovat family and to represent the overall visual colour of the Kellas area. To the Lovat was added a double 'squaring' of darker brown/green to represent the agriculture and a single 'squaring' of yellow brown to represent the presence in the area of several place names containing the gaelic '*buie*' meaning yellow (Bogbuie, Buinach etc). The soils in these places contain natural hydrated iron oxide (ochre), giving rise to a vivid orange colour in boggy areas. The tweed was woven by Kynoch Mill in Keith, now closed.

Kellas was bought and run with Blackhills Estate, Lhanbryde, in 1910. At that time the owner Thomas North Christie used a blue/brown herringbone pattern tweed woven in the border region of Scotland from where he originated. It was felt in the early 1980s that it was no longer suitable, and a new tweed was designed. Tomas Christie and his family now use the 1982 tweed on Brokentore.

Kellas

The tweed was designed in 2006 by the estate owner Frans Jurgens, his wife Hubert and family. The tweed is produced by Johnstons of Elgin.

The tweed has a few special elements: orange yarn from the Netherlands, home country of the Jurgens family; purple yarn for the moors of Kellas; and blue yarn for the River Lossie that runs through the estate. The green colour represents the woods and countryside and makes the tweed blend into the background when worn on the estate.

Kilchoan

Kilchoan is a west coast estate and lies on the Knoydart Peninsula five miles to the east of Mallaig in the area of Loch Nevis. The estate was bought from the Knoydart Peninsula Limited by Mr Eric Delwart who designed the tweed with Hunters of Brora and introduced it in 1988. The makers of the tweed have now changed and the red and yellow stripes are slightly wider apart.

Kilfinichen and Tiroran

The estate lies on the west coast of the Isle of Mull and encompasses the majority of the Ardmeanach Peninsula which stretches westward from the summit of Ben More. The tweed was designed and introduced by Michael and Andrew Holman in 1992 with the help of the artists Brian Rawling and John Wonnacott. The design is a little unusual in its system of overchecks. The estate is significant for its ecological habitat, including unique and rare populations of invertebrates, mammals and birds.

Killiechassie (historical)

The estate of Killiechassie lies about seven miles east of Aberfeldy in Perthshire. The tweed was designed in 1955 by the late Group Captain Hanchet-Taylor who then owned the estate. The tweed is no longer used on the estate. The heathery ground colour is a little unusual and it seems to be based on a tartan design.

Kincardine Castle

The estate lies fifteen miles south-west of Perth beside Auchterarder and belongs to Mr Robert McNeil. In the 13th century the lands were granted to the Grahams, later the Dukes of Montrose. For thirty years from 1770 the estate belonged to Campbell of Glenure and it then passed to William Johnston at the beginning of the 19th century. It was acquired by Mr McNeil in 1990 and the tweed was designed by him and introduced to the estate in 1999.

Kildermorie

The estate is in Easter Ross, lying above a bend of the River Glasa close to Loch Morie and one hour north of Inverness. It can trace a ruined chapel in the glen to 1510. A sheep farm was established at Kildermorie in 1791. In 1912 Charles Dyson Perrins, who owned the neighbouring Ardross estate, bought Kildermorie. Dyson, as he was known, was of the family of Lea & Perrins sauce fame. Dyson was extremely generous to the local community, building a club, which included a library and a reading room, and gifting the Alness Golf Course to the town. In 1994, Mr I and Mrs C Duncan bought what by then was known as Kildermorie North and South Estates. Since then, there has been major investment in a new house, a hydro-electric scheme and the harnessing of natural spring water. Many buildings have been refurbished and restored along with many aspects of the estate. The estate tweed was designed by Mrs Carol Duncan in 2011 and woven by Johnstons of Elgin. The design has vibrant colours of the landscape and subtle lines to incorporate elements of the Duncan tartan.

Kinloch (Sutherland)

Kinloch Estate is by Tongue in the extreme north of Scotland and runs about fifteen miles south from the north coast down the Kyle of Tongue towards Altnaharra. It is owned by Mr Anders Holch Povlsen who bought it from Mr AWG Sykes. The tweed was designed in 1986 by Mr Sykes, helped by his wife Nicola and his aunt, Lady Simon. They used the dominant local colours to produce a good camouflage for the rugged terrain of the area which rises from sea level to more than 3,000 feet at the top of Ben Hope. The estate was purchased from Captain Charles Moncrieff whose family had owned it since 1936.

KINNAIRD

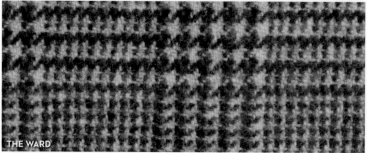

THE WARD

Kinnaird and The Ward

Kinnaird Estate lies seven miles north-west of Dunkeld and was acquired in 1927 by the Hon Lady Ward from the Duke of Atholl. She had the tweed used on the estate designed and made for her by Haggart's of Aberfeldy. When the estate was sold in 2016 the Ward family retained the tweed. The estate is now a commercial sporting estate with five of the estate houses renovated for holiday letting. Kinnaird is now owned by Mr and Mrs Crawford Gillies who have designed their own Kinnaird tweed.

Kinlochewe – including Lochrosque, Cabuie and West Fannich

The estate of Kinlochewe lies at the southern end of Loch Maree and is owned by Mr Pat Wilson who bought Kinlochewe in 1993 from the Whitbread family. Cabuie was bought from another brewery family, The Watneys. The tweed was designed by Mrs Wilson and Haggart's of Aberfeldy. The tweed is in regular use and woven by Glenlyon Tweed Mill.

Kinnell (historical)

Kinnell is near Killin in Perthshire just south of the western end of Loch Tay. Since 1823 the estate has consisted of Kinnell and Auchmore. It used to be owned by JC Macnab of Macnab who designed and introduced the tweed in 1956 with the help of Haggart's of Aberfeldy. The estate has since been broken up. The hill has been given over to forestry.

Kinnordy

The estate is twenty-two miles north of
Dundee, near Kirriemuir, and has been
in the Lyell family since 1781. The tweed
was designed by Campbell's of Beauly
and Lord Lyell's father in about 1937. It is
a variant of the Shepherd Check, having
a green line in the dark colour. Kinnordy
was the home of the eminent geologist Sir
Charles Lyell, who died in 1875.

Kingie

The estate is near Invergarry, Inverness-
shire on the south side of Loch Quoich
and is owned by I & H Brown Ltd. The
estate extends to 17,500 acres. The tweed
was designed by Hunters of Brora in 1995.

Kinrara and Lochindorb

The two estates are near Aviemore, Strathspey. They are owned by the Fletcher family, Kinrara since 2005 and Lochindorb since 2011. The tweed was designed in around 2000 by the owners at that time. The brown replicates bracken, green purple represents heather hills and blue the river Dulnain that runs through the estate. Kinrara belonged to the Duke and Duchess of Gordon in the 1700s. The Duchess of Gordon spent much of her time at Kinrara and was prominent in social and political society. Amongst her many activities was establishing the Gordon Highlanders Regiment. In 1793 the army was short of recruits and the duchess had a bet with the Prince Regent that she could raise more men than he. Her recruiting was unusual to say the least. Wearing a military uniform and a large black feathered hat she toured Scotland, going from marketplace to marketplace, organising reels. Anyone who joined in these reels joined the army and received the King's shilling, the payment received from the Duchess's lips by kissing her. She enrolled 940 men. Upon her death in 1812, the estate passed to her son, George, 5th Duke of Gordon, who was succeeded by the 5th Duke of Richmond whose family owned the estate for more than 100 years. It then passed to Lady Lucy Houston and Sir Steven Bilsland. The tweed is used on both Kinrara and Lochindorb estates and is woven by Glenlyon Tweed Mill.

Kinpurnie

Kinpurnie is six miles from Dundee. Sir James Cayzer Bt designed and introduced the tweed in about 1980. It is a pleasantly simple design which provides good camouflage. The twist of the warp marl produces a slight but noticeable diagonal effect. The estate belonged to Nigel Cayzer who has largely sold it.

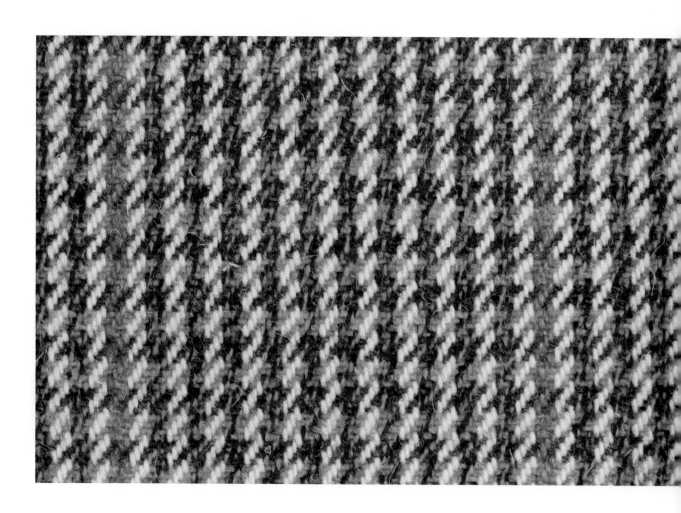

Kintail (historical)

The estate now belongs to the National Trust for Scotland. Kintail is one of the most romantic parts of Scotland, lying to the west of Loch Ness beyond Loch Cluanie on the road to Skye. It is particularly famous for the range of peaks known as the Five Sisters of Kintail. In the first edition of this book, my grandfather-in-law said that he was unable to trace the origins of this tweed and today those working on the estate know nothing about it. The design is certainly one hundred and fifty years old and, as it ties in with the start of estate tweeds, it seems that it was designed for the Kintail estate. It is a standard gun club with a window pane check produced by bordering the dark colour with single threads of red.

Kinpurnie Castle

Kinpurnie Castle is fifteen miles south-west of Forfar in Angus. It is owned by Mr and Mrs Charles Willis. Mrs Willis designed a new tweed, which is loosely based on the older Kinpurnie Castle tweed. The tweed is supplied by Glenlyon Tweed Mill.

Kinpurnie
Castle Estate

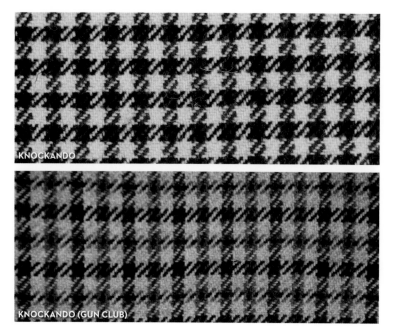
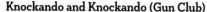

KNOCKANDO

KNOCKANDO (GUN CLUB)

Knockando and Knockando (Gun Club)

The estate is sixteen miles south of Elgin and is the property of Dr Catherine Wills, daughter of Sir David Wills, who bought the estate in the early 1960s in two stages from Major Whitelaw who bought it in 1945. Before that the lands had been owned by the Grants. According to Sandy Milne the retired head ghillie, Major Whitelaw introduced a tweed just after 1945 and probably had it designed and made by Smiths of Knockando, the local mill. For two to three years in the 1970s Martin Wills used the second tweed, the gun club, but he then reverted to the original. The tweed is a straightforward Shepherd Check, black in the weft and dark brown in the warp with a dark green overcheck of the same depth as the ground colours. The gun club has moss-coloured weft check with two threads of green in it. Mr Milne says that when he came to the estate an old retired keeper told him they used to use a brown herringbone tweed which would no doubt also have been made at the local mill. The estate currently has one tweed, Knockando. In 1990 Martin Wills, in conjunction with Hugh Jones of Knockando Woollen Mill, modified the Knockando design to change the weft colours. This is the Knockando shown.

Knockdolian

The Knockdolian tweed was designed and registered in the late 1950s by the 8th Duke of Wellington. The tweed is now used on the Knockdolian Estate, which belong to Lord Richard Wellesley, and on the Bardrochat and Stratfield Saye Estates, owned by the 9th Duke of Wellington.

Lairg

The estate lies on the high ground above the dam on Loch Shin above the town of Lairg. It is owned by Mr James Greenwood. Originally the lands were part of the Sutherland estates but were sold to Sir Edgar Horne in 1920. He in turn sold the estate to Colonel Leslie Bibby in 1960. Mrs Greenwood bought the estate in 1971 and her husband Richard designed the tweed with Pringles of Inverness at that time. The estate was handed down to Mrs Greenwood's son James in 1992. Family members and keepers on Lairg and Balcombe estate in West Sussex wear the tweed. There are rules to the way the tweed is worn. The thin blue line above the brown line and the green line runs vertically.

Langwell and Braemore

Situated on the east coast of Caithness the estate is owned by Welbeck Estates Company Ltd. The estate has been owned by the Duke of Portland family since 1857. The tweed was originally produced on the estate at Ousdale Tweed Mill, which is now closed. The design was 'tweaked' by Lady Anne Cavendish-Bentinck some time between 1976 and 1982 to add in the red line. It is now woven by Johnstons of Elgin.

Laggan, Islay

The estate is located between Bowmore and Port Ellen on the Isle of Islay. It is owned by Laggan Properties Ltd. The tweed was designed by Mrs J Jennings in 1999. It is woven by the Islay Woollen Mill.

Lawers

Lawers Estate is two miles east of the village of Comrie, Perthshire. The tweed was designed by Mr Tom Simpson of Hunters of Brora and was introduced to the estate in 1970. The Mansion House on the estate was designed by Robert Adam.

Lochan and Bandirran

These two estates are both in Perthshire. Bandirran is eight miles north-east of Perth on the Sidlaw hills and Lochan about ten miles south-west of Dunkeld at the head of Strath Braan. They are both managed by Culfargie Estates Ltd which is owned by the Lowson family. The tweed was designed with the help of Hunters of Brora for use on the hill and low ground. Because some tweeds are too dark when wet, the paler background is broken up by the stripes, including the heather colour. The tweed is in regular use and is woven by Johnstons of Elgin.

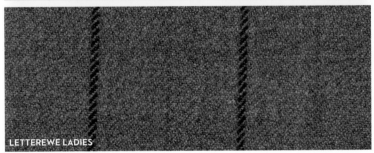

Letterewe and Letterewe (original design)

Letterewe is on the north side of Loch Maree and belongs to the van Vlissingen family who originally bought the Ardlair and Fisherfield portions in 1978. He designed a new tweed for those estates which is now used on the whole estate of Letterewe, the original tweed being discontinued. There are two versions of the tweed, a gentleman's and a lady's. The original design was felt to be too loud but was reserved for the ladies and a quieter version was produced for the men. A length of tweed is presented to any lady who has spent a night at Carnmore, described as the third most remote house in Great Britain. The whole area is known as the last great wilderness. The men's version is illustrated along with the original tweed for which there are no details.

Langwell (Ullapool)

The estate lies some six miles north-east of Ullapool and has belonged to the Dacre family since 2007. The tweed was designed by Hunters of Brora and introduced to the estate in 1962. Until the end of the first world war the estate was part of the Cromarty lands. The design is a gun club on a Lovat ground and a quiet overcheck. The repeat is six centimetres.

Laudale

The estate of Laudale in Morven in Argyllshire, twenty miles north-west of Oban, was bought by the Abel Smith family in 1956. It was then bought by Jonathan Turner in 2013 from the Keith Falconer 1993 Trust. The estate had been part of Glencripesdale Estate, which was broken up after World War II. Much of that estate was bought by the Forestry Commission.

LOCHIEL

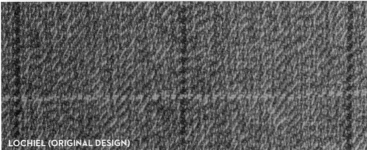

LOCHIEL (ORIGINAL DESIGN)

Lochiel and Lochiel (Original design)

The estate of Achnacarry is at the south
end of the Caledonian Canal near Fort
William. It is owned by Donald Cameron
Younger of Lochiel. There are two slightly
different versions of the estate tweed. The
older was designed and introduced to
the estate by Lochiel and Lady Hermione
Cameron in around 1906. The present
design was introduced by Sir Donald
Cameron of Lochiel. He modified the old
design by introducing a grass green and
Lovat mixture twist into the weft whereas
before the same slack twist of grass green
and fawn had been used in both warp
and weft. The overchecking of scarlet and
yellow remains the same in both designs.

Lochluichart

Situated in Ross-shire near Garve, with
Fannich Ridge on the north-west and
Strathconon on the southern march. It is
owned by Hamish Leslie Melville. The
tweed was designed in the 1920s by the
6th Marquess of Northampton, father of
the current owner's wife. Although a rather
'bright' tweed, the green and gold render it
almost invisible on the Ross-shire hills.

Loch Choire

The estate is a deer forest of 32,000 acres (12,949 hectares) comprising the headwaters of the Naver, Brora and Helmsdale rivers. It was purchased from Sutherland Estates in 1975 by Lord Joicey and Mr Derek Knowles. The estate continued in partnership until it was sold again in 2015. The tweed was designed by Haggart's of Aberfeldy. Sample pieces were spread on the hillside and the one not visible from 300 metres was selected. The idea for the tweed came from the publication of the 1995 edition of this book and also a dissertation at the University of Edinburgh by Rebecca Corbett looking at sociological and traditional aspects of estate tweeds. The dissertation was awarded the highest mark in that year.

Lochbuie

The estate lies at the south-east end of the Isle of Mull and from the 14th century to 1921 it belonged to the MacLaines of Lochbuie. The estate was then sold to Sir Richard Garton in 1922, the great-grandfather of the present owners. The estate is run and farmed by James Corbett and his immediate family. The main interests are sheep and cattle with some stalking. The tweed was designed by Sir Richard Garton and produced by Chalmers of Oban.

Lochmore

Lochmore is in north-west Sutherland, about fifteen miles south-east of Laxford Bridge. It is part of the Reay Forest and is owned by the Grosvenor Estate Trust. The tweed first appeared in one of the Johnstons pattern books more than a hundred and forty-five years ago but there is no record of its origin. It is an attractive form of the gun club or Coigach. A new design from Johnstons was introduced recently.

Lochdochart

The estate is 17 miles north of Loch Lomond and is owned by WJ Christie of Lochdochart OBE. The tweed was designed by Mr Christie and woven by Haggart's of Aberfeldy. On the tweed the black is vertical and the yellow horizontal.

Logie Buchan

Logie is just east of Ellon, fifteen miles north of Aberdeen. It is owned by Mr and Mrs WH Bruce. The tweed was designed by Haggart's of Aberfeldy and introduced to the estate in 1993. The estate is unusual in being formed from a number of properties purchased during the period 1973-94, which reverses the general trend of big estates being broken up into smaller parts. Logie House was built in 1976 and burnt down in 1993 but has now been rebuilt.

Lothian

The Lothian estate lies around the border town of Jedburgh, about thirty miles south-west of Berwick. It is owned by the 13th Marquis of Lothian and his family and the tweed is used on his estate. It was introduced some time before 1969 and was designed by the 12th Marquis of Lothian and Hunters of Brora. The basic design is a variation of the Shepherd Check and the weft overcheck is so quiet that the overall effect is of a red warp stripe.

The Lovat Mixture (historical)

This is one of the first instances of protective colouring and is of great interest to Johnstons of Elgin as it was first woven in our mills. In 1968 Mr ES Harrison wrote: "The present Lord Lovat tells me he has been told that it was first designed by his grandfather for his keepers, ghillies and the family. As a small boy he heard that the idea for the colour came to his grandfather when looking across from the south side of Loch Morar. His grandfather pointed out to his grandmother how the contrasting colours of the primroses and bluebells which were in full bloom on the Lettermorar side blended in with the hill, the white sands of the loch shore, the bracken and the birch trees. From that idea he mixed the tweed for its invisibility on the hill, which was an advantage for sport and deer stalking."

My grandfather-in-law tried to trace its history because it was said the first cloth had been woven at Newmill, but without any success. Then by one of those unbelievable coincidences, when he was in Canada he met an old wool man, Mr Fraser. Mr Fraser said he had worked at the Johnstons mills at Elgin as a boy. He remembered that Lord Lovat had consulted Mr Simon Fraser of Fraser and Smith, his father, who arranged for Johnstons to weave the cloth. After various trials the following mixture emerged as the original Lovat: light blue, thirty-eight parts; bright yellow, sixteen; chrome yellow, twenty-two; dark yellow-brown, twelve; white, twelve. Old Mr Fraser had kept a note of the original mixture although he had only the names and not the samples of the actual colours. These colours are an ingenious analysis of a Highland landscape on a bright spring day.

In the 1960s Mr Campbell of Campbells of Beauly recalled... "my father telling me that my grandfather and the Lord Lovat of that period had some discussions as to the tweed which would be worn by the keepers of the Lovat Estate. I do know that some kind of samples were run out, and were tried at Glen Strathfarrar to see how suitable they would be in matching the hill over which the stalkers would be working." The first piece was woven at Newmill on 26 September 1845 and invoiced to Macdougalls of Inverness on 19 November as 'Lord Lovat's Mixture'. Thereafter the name Lovat appears quite often in the Johnstons books.

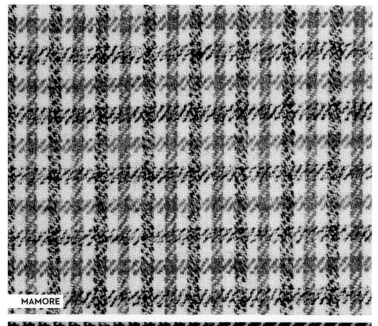

MAMORE

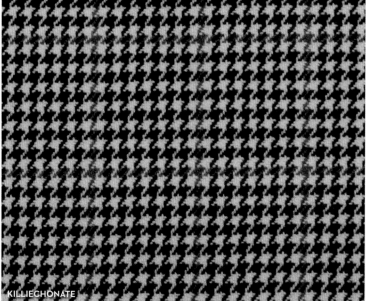

KILLIECHONATE

Mamore and Killiechonate

Situated near Fort William, these two estates cover 79,432 acres. They incorporate 21 'Munros' (hills over 3,000 feet), from the sides of Britain's highest mountain, Ben Nevis (4,409 ft), in the north-west across to Loch Treig in the east and down as far as the Aonach Eagach ridge bordering Glencoe in the south. Both estates have a long sporting history. The main lodge at Killiechonate dates from the 1830s. The ground over the Mamores in the southern half was owned for a long time by the Cameron-Campbell family from the late 19th century who let it out to a number of sporting tenants. The most prominent tenants were the Bibby family who let the estate from 1897 until 1935, entertaining the King in 1909. The deer were driven to him as he lay in ambush by a large boulder above the lodge still known today as 'The King's Butt'.

The Cameron-Campbells sold the estates to the North British Aluminium Company in 1935, at which stage they, along with Killiechonate, became permanently attached to the aluminium smelting operations at Fort William and, up until 2000, at Kinlochleven. The company and therefore the estates, changed hands a number of times and, ultimately, were sold by Rio Tinto Alcan to the current owners in December 2016, subsidiaries of the Gupta Family Group Alliance. The estates are the rainfall catchment areas for the hydro-electric schemes at Kinlochleven and Fort William. The two hydro-electric schemes generate power required for the aluminium smelter at Fort William which employs 170 people, soon to be several hundred more under the new ownership.

There used to be tweeds for both Killiechonate and Mamore, which fell into abeyance for many years with the stalkers using the British Alcan Tweed, now only in use at Glenshero (page 88). However, the Guptas are now reinstating both of these older more traditional patterns for the individual estates. Both are woven by Johnstons of Elgin.

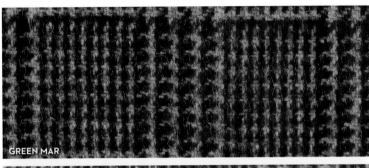

GREEN MAR

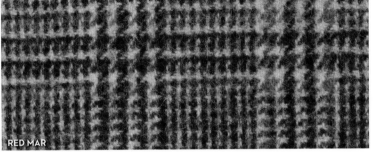

RED MAR

Mar

Mar lies four miles west of Braemar. Strictly speaking Mar has two tweeds, the Green Mar and the Red Mar. The whole estate was originally owned by the Duchess of Fife. On her death it was passed to her nephew, Captain Ramsay of Mar, and it was split in 1960. Captain Ramsay kept the southern portion which is now in a trust and run by his son-in-law, Captain Mark Nicolson of Cairnbulg Castle. Before 1960 the family used to wear the Green Mar and the keepers and ghillies the Red Mar. When the estate was divided, the Ramsays retained the Green Mar for their estate, now called Mar. The other part is now Mar Lodge and is owned by the National Trust for Scotland. They use Red Mar tweed, woven by Glenlyon Tweed Mill. Tradition has it that the Green Mar was designed by King Edward VII when, as Prince of Wales, he used to shoot from Geldie Lodge, which is in the Forest of Mar.

Meggernie and Lochs

The estates, located in Glenlyon, are owned by Mrs BJ Malim and a family trust. Together they extend to just under 40,000 acres and provide excellent stalking in spectacular countryside.

Mrs Bevs Malim inherited Meggernie from her mother, Mrs Donald Searle, in 1995, having already acquired neighbouring Lochs Estate.

Meggernie Castle was built in 1585 by Colin Campbell. Successive Campbells owned the property, including Robert Campbell, leader of the Glencoe massacre. They were followed by the Menzies of Culdares family. In the 1880s Meggernie was bought by John Bullough, who also owned Kinloch Castle on the Isle of Rhum. His son (George) sold the estate to Sir Edward Wills Bt in the 1920s and subsequently his son, Sir Edward Wills Bt, sold the estate to Mrs Donald Searle in 1979. The current tweed was designed by Mrs Donald Searle in collaboration with P & J Haggart in 1979. It is now woven by Glenlyon Tweed Mill, Aberfeldy.

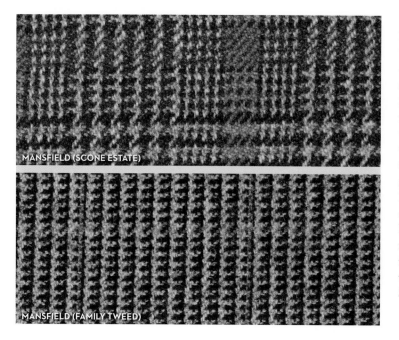

MANSFIELD (SCONE ESTATE)

MANSFIELD (FAMILY TWEED)

Mansfield (Scone Estate) and Mansfield (family tweed)

The estate lies north of Perth, at Scone on the east bank of the River Tay and is owned by the Rt Hon The Earl of Mansfield. It has belonged to his family for more than 400 years. There are two versions of the estate tweed. The Glenurquhart check is used regularly on the estate and was designed by the Earl's grandmother, Dorothea, 7th Countess of Mansfield in 1965. The other version was designed again by the Earl's grandmother but earlier in 1949 and is worn by members of the family. It is based on the bi-coloured wool of Jacob sheep which used to be kept in the park at Scone Palace.

Milton of Blairquhan

Milton of Blairquhan is six miles east of Maybole in Ayrshire and has been owned by the Hunter Blair family for more than two hundred years. The tweed was introduced by Sir Edward Hunter Blair, 4th Bt, in about 1860, but after some years it fell into disuse. The design was reintroduced by James Hunter Blair, copied from a cap given to him by Miss Campbell, daughter of a former head gamekeeper. Sadly, there is no information on the origins of the original tweed which is a simple gun club. The present owners are Sir Patrick and Lady Hunter Blair.

North Uist

North Uist Estate is in the Outer Hebrides and belongs to the North Uist Estates Trust 1990. A previous owner was the Duke of Hamilton who sold to Earl and Countess Granville in 1960. The tweed was commissioned in the 1960s and designed by Peggy Macdonald, Locheport, North Uist. It is in use today.

Otter

Otter is on the Cowal Peninsula in Argyll, twenty-five miles west of Glasgow. It is the property of Mr NKS Wills, having previously belonged to the Rankin family. The tweed was designed by Haggart's of Aberfeldy and introduced to the estate in 1992. The overchecking on the moss-coloured ground is very quiet, two single orange threads in the warp and two single blue threads flanking a pair of moss-coloured threads in the weft.

Phoines

The estate is on the east side of the A9 road between Newtonmore and Dalwhinnie. It is the property of the Hon Michael J Samuel and the tweed was designed and introduced by the Hon Mrs PM Samuel. Woven by Glenlyon Tweed Mill.

Pitcastle

The estate lies in Strathtay, ten miles north-west of Dunkeld and is owned by Mr Struan Robertson, previously owned by Tate & Lyle, the sugar company. It was bought in 1989 from the Kyd family. The tweed was designed and chosen by Lady Pixie Shaw, wife of the Chairman, following comments by the factor, Mr Macdonald, that many Scottish estates had their own distinctive tweeds, notably the neighbouring estate of Kinnaird.

Portmore

Portmore is one of the Border estates and lies about ten miles north of Peebles. It is presently owned by Mr and Mrs David Reid who bought it from Mr John Robertson. The estate has been unlucky in that Portmore House has twice been burned down, once in the 1860s and again in 1986. The tweed was introduced in 1993 and was designed by Haggart's of Aberfeldy. Portmore has beautiful gardens which are open to the public.

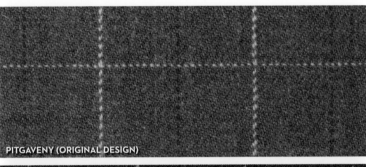

PITGAVENY (ORIGINAL DESIGN)

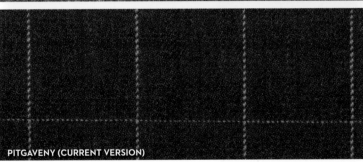

PITGAVENY (CURRENT VERSION)

Pitgaveny (original design) and Pitgaveny (current version)

The estate lies three miles east of Elgin and belongs to Crinan Dunbar and his sister Mrs R Russell. It has been owned by the Brander and Dunbar families since 1765. The designer of the tweed is not known but the use of the Dunbar heraldic colours, gules and argent (red and white) on the overcheck suggests that Sir AH Dunbar, Bt, 1828-1910, had a hand in it. The design was probably introduced by Captain James Dunbar Brander who owned the estate from 1869 to 1902, when he was succeeded by his son Captain James Brander Dunbar, based on John Buchan's *John Macnab*. The ground colour varies from green to lovat depending on the mixtures available at the mill making it and it is excellent camouflage in the Laich of Moray or on the hill. The second design illustrated is an example of an old pattern and shows how colours can change over the years. For many years the tweed was made by the Menzies mill in the village of Dallas in Moray, after which the great city of Dallas in Texas is named. But this mill closed down and the manufacture was transferred to Johnstons of Elgin who made the first design illustrated above. The change of colour due to a change of manufacturer is fairly common among estate tweeds but the change in the size of the overchecking is most unusual.

John Macnab

In 1925, Lord Tweedsmuir, writing as John Buchan, penned a novel titled *John Macnab*. Macnab's claim to fame was the ability to shoot a stag, catch a salmon and shoot a brace of grouse all in the same day without being caught by a gamekeeper. The idea for using this fictional character's exploits as a real challenge was subsequently proposed by Lord Tweedsmuir's friend, James Brander Dunbar of Pitgaveny. Dunbar himself achieved a 'Macnab' after accepting a bet from a fellow volunteer army officer that he could not bag a stag without being caught. The army officer lost the bet and Dunbar received a cheque for £20 on 4 November 1897. It was addressed to 'J.B. Dunbar, poacher'. Dunbar had poached the stag three days after the estate owners were warned that he would try. He was also successful in catching the salmon and grouse within the same 24 hours. The salmon, grouse and stag were all returned to the relevant estate owners. For many years Lord Tweedsmuir stalked and fished on Ardtornish Estate, on which the fictitious estate in the book is based.

When Lord Tweedsmuir was appointed Governor General of Canada, James Brander Dunbar addressed his letter of congratulations to 'My Dear John Macnab'. Pitgaveny Estate still retains an autographed copy of Lord Tweedsmuir's book inscribed 'John Macnab from John Buchan, 4/8/25'.

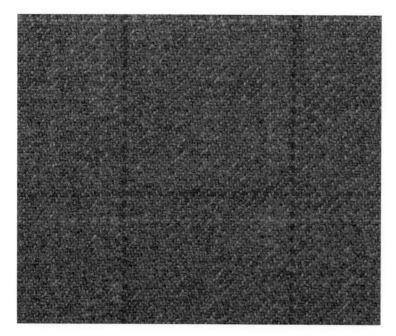

Reay (historical)

Reay, like Lochmore, is in north-west Sutherland, twenty miles south-south-east of Cape Wrath. It is a large and desolate area owned by the Grosvenor Estate Trusts. Like the Lochmore tweed there is no information on who designed this pattern nor when it was introduced but it is thought to have been selected by the 2nd Duke of Westminster some time after 1919. It is not used at present.

Remony

The estate is situated on the south-east shore of Loch Tay in Perthshire. It is owned by James Duncan Millar. His grandfather, Sir James Duncan Millar, an Edinburgh lawyer, had been a sporting tenant for a couple of years before he bought the estate from the Executors of the Earl of Breadalbane in 1925. The tweed was designed by his mother, Mrs Louise Duncan Millar, in 1946. Working with Haggart's of Aberfeldy she chose the blue-ish pattern as she liked the colour. Also, it was different from other estate tweeds. In reality it is a wonderful tweed which blends easily into the countryside whether grass, rushes, rock or woods. It is still worn to this day and is supplied by Glenlyon Tweed Mill.

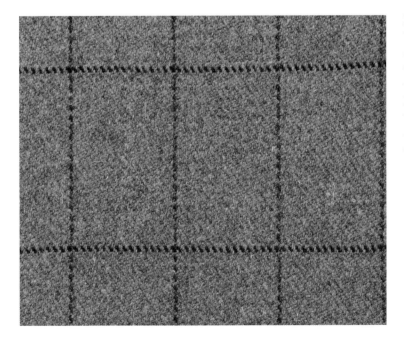

Roro

The estate is situated in Glenlyon. It is owned by The Hon Emily Astor. The tweed was designed by her in 2000 and woven by Glenlyon Tweed Mill. The estate borders Ben Lawers. At nearby Fortingale village there's a yew tree that is more than 2,000 years old and reputed to be the oldest living tree in Britain.

Rossal and Ardvergnish

The estate sits at the head of Loch Scridain on the Isle of Mull and rises from sea level to the top of Ben More at 3,169 feet. It is owned by the Timothy Laing Family Fund, which acquired it in 1990. The tweed is a copy of a similar one believed to have been made for David Lumsden in the 1930s. The current tweed is a superb interpretation by the Isle of Mull Weavers and was designed by Rob Ryan. The tweed is widely used today.

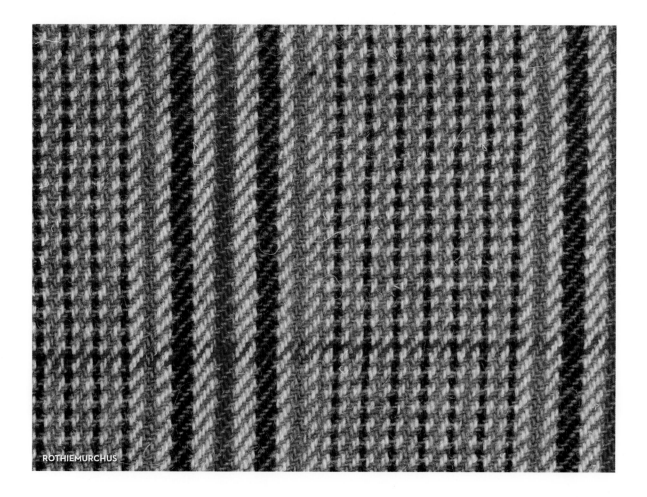

ROTHIEMURCHUS

Sannox

The estate lies in the north-east of the Isle of Arran in the estuary of the River Clyde and is the property of Mr CJG Fforde. The tweed was designed by Haggart's of Aberfeldy in conjunction with Mr Fforde and introduced to the estate in 1975 for the stalkers' suits. A lighter weight of the same pattern has been used for interior design both on the estate and in a prestigious Edinburgh hotel. After several experiments, the best blend to merge with the local 'hill' autumn colours came about with the inclusion of two pink (strangely enough!) threads between the double maroon lines in the weft and also flanking them.

ROTHIEMURGUS (ORIGINAL DESIGN)

Rothiemurchus and Rothiemurcus (original design)

The estate lies across the River Spey from Aviemore and has been loved and cared for by the Grants of Rothiemurchus for eighteen generations. There is evidence of hut circles and a fort from the Bronze Age, and Rothiemurchus was 'held' by several owners until 1542 when it passed to John Grant, 4th of Freuchie, son of the Chief of Grant and his son Patrick Grant of Muckerach – 'gin he could win it'. Elizabeth Grant's book *Memoirs of a Highland Lady* describes life on Rothiemurchus in the early 1800s. The high ground of the estate takes in some of the high tops of the Cairngorms. The current tweed was designed by the present owner, John Grant of Rothiemurchus, DL, his family and stalker in the 1980s and the colours were updated by Haggart's of Aberfeldy in 1993.

Scatwell and Cabaan

Scatwell lies in the glen of the River Conon, twenty miles north-west of Inverness. It now belongs to Earl of Aylesford, formerly Lord Guernsey. The estate was purchased in 1990 from Mr Macdonald-Buchanan of Strathconon. Lord and Lady Guernsey designed a new tweed for the estate, which is now known as Scatwell and Cabaan.

Seaforth (historical)

Loch Seaforth is on the east coast of the Isle of Lewis in the Outer Hebrides. There is no history of this design and it is really a Mackenzie tweed but it was adopted and used by the Seaforth Highlanders as a regimental tweed for the commissioned ranks of the regiment and presumably is still used by members of that regiment. Perhaps this adoption is not surprising when one remembers that the regiment was raised by Kenneth Mackenzie, Earl of Seaforth. The pattern appears in the Johnstons pattern books of more than a century ago. It is a beautiful scheme of two shades of brown on a white ground with a dull russet overcheck. The design is a standard gun club.

The Shepherd Check (historical)

Strictly speaking the Shepherd Check is not an estate tweed but, as it was the foundation of the first and many other estate tweed designs, it has been included as the first generic pattern. It is known the world over and is simply a small black-and-white check of about six threads of black and six of white. There is no definite standard. It was the traditional tweed of the Border shepherds and this was the design that Miss Balfour embellished with the scarlet overcheck to create the Glenfeshie mixture in around 1840. It was said that Miss Balfour introduced this check to match the grey and red granite of Glenfeshie but another, possibly more likely version, has it that the purpose was to distinguish the men of the forest from the shepherds.

Shielbridge

The estate is owned by the Shielbridge Trust and is situated near the village of Acharacle, Argyll, at the west end of Loch Shiel, Inverness-shire. The tweed was designed in 1937 by the Hon Mrs AM Holman. Shielbridge was formerly part of Ardnamurchan Estate, the most westerly point on the British mainland. In times gone by it was owned by the MacIans, a sept of the Macdonalds, Lords of the Isles, who lost it to the 5th Earl of Argyll, Chief of Clan Campbell. It was farmed for deer, for in 1493 and 1495 King James IV of Scotland came to hunt. In 1897 it was bought by Charles Dunell Rudd, a business associate of Cecil Rhodes and a director of De Beers. The next owner was Kenneth M Clark (Baron Clark 1903-1983), the famous art historian. In 1993 his executors sold the Shielbridge portion to Lady Trent of the Boots the Chemist family from whom the present owners are descended.

Snaigow and Glenquaich

Snaigow estate lies a few miles east of Dunkeld and Glenquaich is about the same distance to the west. Both have belonged to Cadogan family interests since 1940. It is not known who designed the estate tweed but it was introduced by Lord Cadogan in the 1960s. It is a variation of the Shepherd Check and deliberately covers the colour requirements of a low ground and moorland estate.

South Chesthill

This estate is in Glenlyon, which lies in Perthshire to the west of Aberfeldy. Chesthill Estate can trace its origins to Campbell ownership from the 1500s to 1700. Robert Campbell, the 5th Laird of Glenlyon (1630-1696) lived at Chesthill House at the time he led the detachment of government troops responsible for the infamous Glencoe Massacre of the MacDonalds of Glencoe in 1691. Since then it has passed through the hands of two Menzies families, Sir Donald Currie and his descendants who split the estate into North and South in 1949, and the Roy family. The present owners of South Chesthill, the Ramsay family, bought it in 1978 and have expanded it to some 7,000 acres and roughly six miles of fishing. It is used as a family home and is also available for sporting lets. The tweed was designed by Haggart's of Aberfeldy, introduced to the estate in 1980 and now woven by Glenlyon Tweed Mill.

Strathallan

The estate lies a few miles to the south-west of Auchterarder and is the property of the Roberts family following the death of Sir William Denby Roberts, Bt. Before Sir William the estate belonged to Lord Perth but there is no information on who designed the tweed nor when it was introduced to the estate.

Struy

The estate lies about twenty miles west-south-west of Inverness and is owned by the Spencer-Nairn family. It was originally part of the Lovat estates and was sold to Colonel Cooper about 1920 and was then bought by Sir Robert Spencer-Nairn in 1934. When Sir Robert died his two sons inherited and the estate was divided in half along the line of the River Farrar. The northern half, owned by Frank C Spencer-Nairn, is called Culligran and the southern half, owned by Angus Spencer-Nairn, is still called Struy. Both estates use the same tweed, which has been worn on the estate since 1934 but there is no information on the designer or the date of introduction.

Strathconon and Scardroy

Strathconon lies in the area fifteen to twenty miles west of Muir of Ord. The estate was purchased by the Christiansen family from the Macdonald-Buchanans early in 1995. Before that it belonged to the Combe family and before that Lord Balfour. The tweed now in use is the tweed designed by the Hon, Lady Macdonald-Buchanan for the neighbouring estate of Scatwell in 1953. When the Macdonald-Buchanans sold Scatwell to Lord and Lady Guernsey they retained the design of the Scatwell tweed for use on their Strathconon estates. Over the years the colours of this tweed have altered slightly and the present version is rather more yellow than the original. (See also Scatwell and Cabaan, page 131.)

Scardroy was purchased by the Laing family in 1987 from Peter Combe. The Scardroy tweed was designed by Murdoch Laing in 1994. It is used occasionally. The estate was sold to the Christiansen family in 2013 and the Strathconon tweed is now used on both estates.

Strathconon (old design)

The original Strathconon tweed illustrated here is unusual as it is a plain diamond of eight by eight threads. Mr Peter Combe said the tweed was introduced by his grandfather in around 1909 but there is also a story that Lord Balfour, who owned the estate before the Combe family, dressed the troops of his regiment in the same tweed. The tweed was woven by the local weaver George MacIver in Dingwall High Street. Mr Combe has had in his possession a collection of patterns of the tweed showing slight variations in shade and colour which he found among his grandfather's belongings. He said his grandfather sent his men up the hill carrying the tweed while he spied them through his glass to see which pattern was the most invisible.

Tarbert

The estate lies on the Isle of Jura which is nearly cut in half by Loch Tarbert. It is the property of Viscount Astor who introduced the tweed to the estate in 1966. It was designed by Sarah Baring, Viscount Astor's mother. The weft element in the overcheck is subtle against the component colours of the background.

Tillypronie

The estate of Tillypronie is near Tarland in Aberdeenshire, thirty miles west of Aberdeen, and was owned by the Hon Philip Astor. The tweed was introduced by his father, the Hon Gavin Astor, who designed it in 1951. The general effect is of very dark heather. The overcheck on the warp is of two threads, green representing the woods and yellow for the arable land, and in the weft the overcheck is a similar two threads, dark blue for the river and light blue for the sky on a herringboned ground. The estate was sold in early 2017 but the owner is unknown.

Tulchan Speyside (historical)

Tulchan is about nine miles north of Grantown-on-Spey and was once part of the Seafield lands. It had been owned by Mr and Mrs L Litchfield since October 1993, now Tulchan Sporting Estates Ltd. In March 2017 the estate was sold to a company controlled by Mr Yuri Shefler. There is no information on who designed the tweed or when it was introduced but it is no longer in use on the estate.

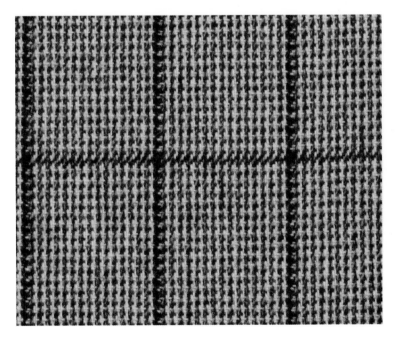

Tulchan of Glenisla

Located in the Angus Glens, Tulchan of Glenisla and neighbouring Balmoral, Invercauld and Airlie all work together to manage deer herds in a sustainable and professional manner. The estate is owned by Tulchan of Glenisla Forest Ltd. Lord Inchcape acquired the estate in the early 1900s. He worked with Johnstons in the 1920s to design the tweed which has brown of the heather and yellow to light brown of the patches of grass. Johnstons of Elgin produce the cloth to this day. It is used on the estate.

Urrard (historical)

Urrard is two miles north-west of Pitlochry on the site of the Battle of Killiecrankie. The original Urrard House dates back to 1681 and the Battle of Killiecrankie was fought on 27 July 1689. Mr Andrew Mackinnon bought the estate from Mr Charles Findlay in 1988. Mr Mackinnon designed and introduced the tweed to the estate in 1989. The estate is currently owned by Mrs Bridget Price and her son Daniel Price. They purchased it in 2013 from Ms Vanessa Harryhausen.

Urlar

The estate is near Aberfeldy, Perthshire and is owned by Mr Donald Ogilvy Watson. It is an upland estate on the hills to the south of the Tay valley near Kenmore and Aberfeldy. The tweed is supplied by Glenlyon Tweed Mill.

Wemyss and March

The Wemyss and March estates, with lands in East Lothian, Peeblesshire, Selkirkshire and Gloucestershire, are all administered by The Wemyss and March Estates Management Company Limited whose chairman is the Earl of Wemyss. The tweed is used throughout the estates in Scotland. It has a very simple pattern, and the ground colour is very similar to the mixture, called 'Hodden Grey', produced in 1859 for the London Scottish Regiment by Lord Elcho, who succeeded to the title of 9th Earl of Wemyss and March in 1883. Hodden Grey is thought to have been the first neutral regimental uniform in the world. The white check is very prominent and overshadows the single thread of mid-blue alongside it.

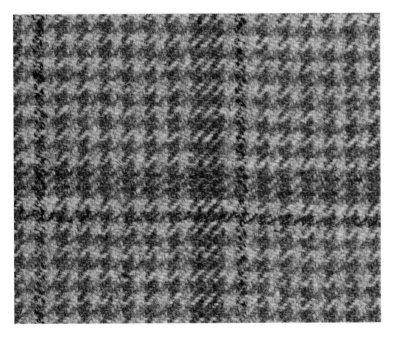

West Monar and Pait

The estate takes in the west end of Loch Monar which lies thirty-five miles or so due west from Inverness. It is owned by the Stroyan family who bought it from Captain RKW Stirling in 1965. The tweed was designed by Mr CSR Stroyan and Campbells of Beauly and has been used since 1966. The lodge at Pait can only be reached by boat down Loch Monar and is one of the most remote in Scotland.

SCOTTISH REGIMENTS AND ENGLISH ESTATES

The original 1968 book on Scottish Estate Tweeds described them as 'Scottish District Checks', and author ES Harrison included a chapter on tweeds that are of a similar style. These include tweeds adopted by our regiments and those used by estates in England. We have included a small selection as they show how they are derived from the original tweeds. Their purpose is very similar to tweeds – being functional clothing in the outdoors and in most cases a form of camouflage. In addition they identify a wearer as belonging to a particular place or organisation.

The Black Watch

The tweed was designed by officers of the 3rd (Militia) Battalion The Black Watch prior to 1914. In 1915, the 42nd Battalion Royal Highlanders of Canada (Black Watch) was formed. Because of the mobilisation of such a large number of men the Commanding Officer, Lieutenant Colonel GS Cantlie, had the idea of having tweed for the uniforms woven in Canada. Perhaps this did not happen as an order was placed with Johnstons of Elgin. This was one of the few cargoes lost to enemy action. A replacement order arrived safely. The tweed was turned into glengarries and kilts and the tweed harmonised well with khaki tunics of wartime. This example of ordering tweed from Scotland was followed by Lt-Col P Davidson who was commanding the newly formed 73rd Battalion, Royal Highlanders of Canada (Black Watch). His order was for 3,000 yards and a width of 58 inches.

The tweed is a lovat mixture overchecked by a group of colours and must be made up with the blue line of the overcheck uppermost and with the colours used being regimental colours of blue over red over green. In our specification of 1916 the colours are described as Canadian lovat, beech green, crimson and lavender blue. The tweed is still worn by officers who served in the Black Watch (Royal Highland Regiment). The regiment was raised in 1739 and was the senior Highland Regiment and was numbered the 42nd Regiment of Foot for most of its existence. In 2006 after 267 years' service to the Crown, the regiment was merged into the newly formed Royal Regiment of Scotland. The Black Watch, 3rd Battalion, the Royal Regiment of Scotland now carries forward the traditions of the "gallant Forty Twa".

The Highlanders

In 1994 and 1995 Lt-Col the Hon HBHE Monro, Commanding Officer, The Highlanders (Seaforth, Gordons and Camerons) and a small committee worked with Hugh Jones at Knockando Woollen Mill to design this tweed. The tweed derives from the regimental tweeds of the Queen's Own Highlanders (Seaforth and Camerons), which is green/silver background with a blue and white stripe, and the Gordon Highlanders, which is a green background with a green and yellow stripe. The Highlanders amalgamated on 28 March 2006 to become The Highlanders, 4th Battalion The Royal Regiment of Scotland (4 SCOTS). The tweed is worn widely by ex-servicemen and those serving in 4 SCOTS today.

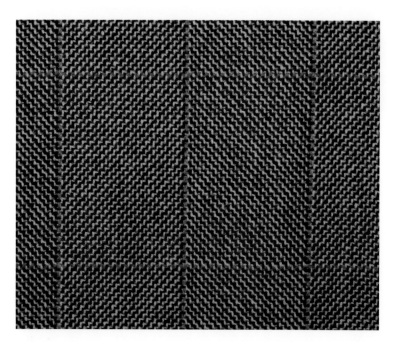

The Royal Scots Dragoon Guards

The right to wear this tweed, made exclusively for the regiment, was passed to the officers of the Scots Greys (restyled The Royal Scots Greys in 1921) by HRH Prince Arthur of Connaught whose family tweed it was. Prince Arthur, a grandson of Queen Victoria, served in the regiment from 1907-1914 and was its Colonel-in-Chief from 1921-1938. The Royal Scots Greys amalgamated with the 3rd Carabiniers in 1971 and formed The Royal Scots Dragoon Guards. Officers of the regiment continue to wear this tweed today.

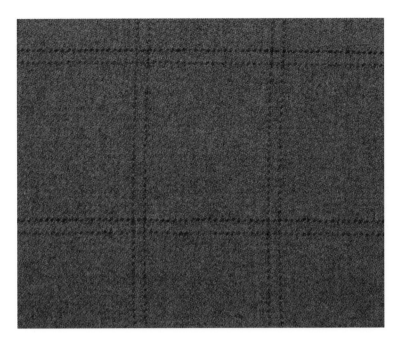

The Royal Regiment of Scotland

The tweed was created in 2006 after the amalgamation of the Scottish Infantry Regiments to create The Royal Regiment of Scotland. The tweed was designed and approved by a committee of senior officers within the regiment and by the Colonel of the Regiment, Lt Gen Andrew Graham. The tweed is worn by officers and soldiers of the regiment. The regiment has seven battalions of which two are shown in this book.

Aldbourne Chase

Situated in Wiltshire, Aldbourne Chase sits on the rolling downs where John O'Gaunt chased deer in the 1300s. Johnstons of Elgin worked with Aldbourne to design a striking tweed to reflect aspects of the Wiltshire Downs: the blue sky, the yellow of the wheat straw, the red of the castle and the white of the chalk downs on a light olive green background. The tweed works well on the estate, the colours fitting for this estate and different from those found in Scotland.

Holkham

Holkham is in North Norfolk and is owned by the Earl of Leicester. The tweed was developed in 2003 by the Earl of Leicester's wife, the Countess of Leicester, working with Johnstons of Elgin to redesign the previous tweed. Lady Leicester thought the brown-green hue would be appropriate for the Norfolk landscape in winter with its ploughed fields and woodland. The dark line in the tweed picks up the colour of the Keeper's bowler hats and the orange lines give warmth. The tweed is used today in three-piece suits tailored by George Goddard Ltd, worn with Holkham Bowler Hats on shoot days. Holkham Hall is one of England's finest examples of the Palladian style of architecture. It was built in the 18th century.

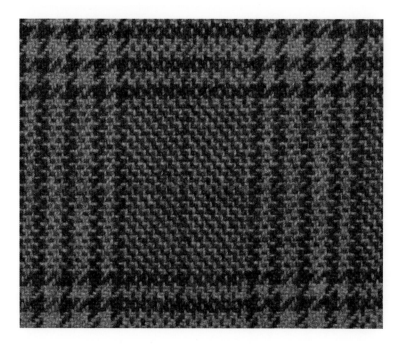

Kelling

The estate is owned by Mr and Mrs G Widdowson and it is situated on the North Norfolk coast near Holt. Nearby estates include Blickling, Holkham and Sandringham. The estate owns the appropriately named 'The Pheasant' hotel.

Kelling Hall was built in 1913 for Henri Deterding, one of the Founders of Shell, the Royal Dutch Petroleum Company. The hall is noted as being the first design by the architect Sir Edward Maufe. The hall is based on a butterfly plan. The tweed is produced by Johnstons of Elgin and tailored by George Goddard Ltd. The tweed is in regular use.

Wilton

Wilton House and Estate covers 14,000 acres near Salisbury, Wiltshire. Wilton is owned by Lord and Lady Pembroke, the 18th Earl and Countess. It has been owned by their family, the 1st Earl of Pembroke, since 1547. Wilton House stands pre-eminent in the art history of England. It has been regularly open to the public since the early 1700s. The tweed was designed by Lady Pembroke in 2012 and it is woven by Glenlyon Tweed Mill.

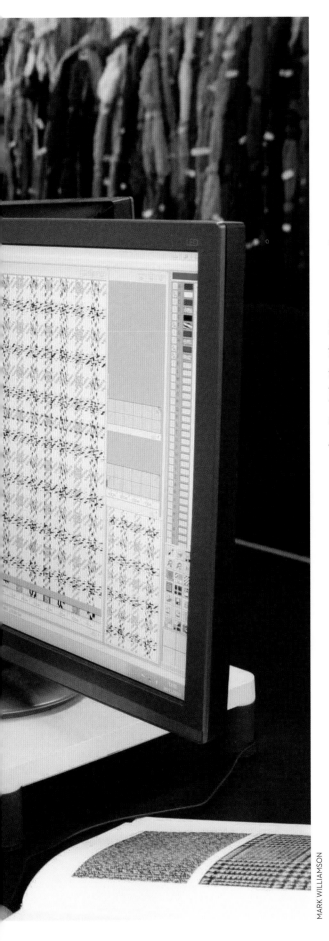

MARK WILLIAMSON

PROCESSING AN ESTATE TWEED

Since the mid-nineteenth century, technology has changed and improved the production of estate tweeds but the basic steps remain the same: dyeing, carding, spinning, weaving and finishing. Johnstons of Elgin follow this procedure.

DESIGN

Every order for estate tweed begins in the Johnstons design studio. If clients reorder their usual tweed, checks are made on colour availability to see if more yarn is needed or if additional wool needs to be dyed.

Other clients may want to replicate an item of clothing or modify an old design. Often new ideas are developed by consulting the company's extensive archive.

In all cases, the designers work with the client using computer-aided design. Ideas are generated and then printed out for approval and/or adjustment. If further investigation is needed, a small sample is woven to check the colour.

The design shown here is the tweed from Mamore Estate, north of Fort William overlooking Loch Ness.

WOOL STORE

Estate tweeds are made from 100 per cent wool, which has the level of wear and performance required for the outdoors. It is an excellent insulator: it's cool to the touch and retains heat. Wool is also water repellent, hard-wearing and comfortable.

MARK WILLIAMSON

DYE HOUSE

Johnstons has a dyeing palette of more than 7,500 colours, including 350 classics that are used for regular customers.

Scottish dyeing is traditionally done before carding and spinning, and Johnstons produces eight tons of dyed fibre using this method every week. They also dye wool by the hank, a more gentle process which is used for dyeing small amounts of yarn for a woven stripe.

For commercial reasons, the company uses only environmentally friendly synthetic dyes and disposes of dye liquor in an effluent tank that is diluted and balanced out for an acceptable pH level. Such practice has earned them quality ratings from the International Standard Organisation.

TWISTING

After dyeing, carding and spinning the wool, the thread is twisted in preparation for weaving. Although the Mamore estate tweed seems like it only has two colours (grey and white), there are actually four – off-white, grey, black and red.

Some of the tweed mixtures consist of up to eight different colours, which are twisted into two-ply yarns in preparation for weaving. The light twist of the yarn gives the completed fabric its strength and durability.

MARK WILLIAMSON

IAN URQUHART

WARPING

Prior to weaving, the warp for the Mamore tweed is placed on
a drum. Johnstons uses two different warping machines for their tweed:
either the UK-made Hattersley or this German-made Karl Mayer. The
warp runs the length of the cloth and the weft lies along the width.

IAN URQUHART

WEAVING

The simplest form of weaving involves interlacing two sets of threads using an over-one, under-one motion. The weaving of cloth for estate tweeds, however, follows a more traditional Scottish structure called the 2 x 2 weave. To achieve a heavier and more dense cloth, yarns cross over two and under two.

Johnstons has a mixture of 18 dobby and seven Jacquard looms in its Elgin mill. Because they are woven in straight lines, most estate tweeds and tartans are made on dobby looms. The dobby is a mechanism on top of the loom. It controls the lifting and lowering of the shafts, allowing the shuttle carrying the weft yarn to move back and forth across the warp.

This rapier loom made by Dornier in Germany operates slightly differently. Weft yarn is carried halfway across the warp by a thin rod, after which it hands the yarn to another rapier to move it to the other side. Cloth that requires weaving shapes is done on the more complex Jacquard looms.

DARNING

Once the weaving process is completed the cloth is
inspected and any imperfections are corrected by darning.

IAN URQUHART

MARK WILLIAMSON

FINISHING STAGE ONE

The first stage in the finishing process involves scouring the cloth in warm water and mild soap. This removes most of the oils that are naturally present in sheep's wool. The process helps to break up the fibres and soften their appearance.

This traditional wooden dolly is being loaded with two 60-metre (196.85 feet) lengths of Mamore estate tweed that have been stitched together. During the washing and subsequent drying process, the cloth will shrink from 170 centimetres (66.92 inches) to 150 centimetres (59.05 inches) in width.

STAGE TWO

A Stenter drying machine holds the cloth in place with tenterhooks to ensure the finished width is maintained while being heated, hence the phrase "to be on tenterhooks". The machine ensures the tweed is kept to its finished width and remains straight with no distortion to the design.

IAN URQUHART

IAN URQUHART

STAGES THREE AND FOUR

After drying, estate tweed is fed into this Italian-made Vapodec machine. It uses steam
to prepare the cloth for its final permanent finish, which is carried out in a Decatiser.

IAN URQUHART

STAGE FIVE

As the finished cloth is put on a roll,
it is inspected to ensure quality.

INDEX

NORTH UIST